Stillwater, Minnesota
A Photographic History

Minnesota-Wisconsin interstate lift bridge at Stillwater. November 17, 1990, *Dean R. Thilgen.*

The bridge has become a modern symbol of Stillwater. Completed in 1931, the lift bridge was the first not made of wood. It stands as one of the last of its kind and is on the National Register of Historic Places. In the summer months, the lift section raises for large boats to pass underneath. This creates traffic jams at each end of the bridge. The Minnesota and Wisconsin transportation departments have prepared plans for a new bridge. The future of the present bridge is uncertain.

1843-1993

Stillwater, Minnesota
A Photographic History

Brent T. Peterson and Dean R. Thilgen

Valley History Press
Stillwater, Minnesota

FRONT COVER: St. Croix River at Stillwater. October 7, 1990, *Dean R. Thilgen.*
The St. Croix River is a source of pride for the residents of Stillwater. This view is from Pioneer Park, named for Isaac Staples, one of the many lumbermen from Stillwater's past. His prominent Italianate home formerly occupied the park site. Staples' sawmill was located below at the foot of the bluff.

BACK COVER: Sesquicentennial seal.
Based on the original Stillwater city seal, Ed Hochsford designed this seal in honor of Stillwater's 150th anniversary.

Sources of photographs are cited on page 112-113.

Copyright ©1992 by Brent T. Peterson and Dean R. Thilgen. All Rights Reserved.

Published by Valley History Press, P.O. Box 590, Stillwater, Minnesota, 55082.

Book design and photographic digitization by Dean R. Thilgen.

PRINTED IN THE UNITED STATES OF AMERICA

December 1992

International Standard Book Number 0-9634842-0-6

ABOUT THE AUTHORS

Brent T. Peterson is employed by the Minnesota Historical Society as a site interpreter. He is a past co-director of the St. Croix County Historical Society of Hudson, Wisconsin. Peterson specializes in regional baseball history and he plans to publish a work on this subject. A 1982 graduate of Stillwater High School, Peterson has a bachelor's degree from Mankato State University.

Dean R. Thilgen is employed by Kinko's of Minnesota, Inc. as a Macintosh computer support specialist. He was graduated from Stillwater High School in 1982 and has a B.S. in Mass Communication from Bemidji State University. St. Croix Valley railroad history is Thilgen's specialty and he plans to revise and expand a previous work on the subject through Valley History Press. Thilgen is also a volunteer for the *Minnesota Genealogist,* the quarterly journal of the Minnesota Genealogical Society. A genealogist since 1981, Dean has researched his family's history at libraries, archives, courthouses, cemeteries and historic sites in six states and the District of Columbia.

To All Who Know, Respect and
Enjoy Local History

Contents

TO THE
A D M I R E R S
OF

FINE
PICTURES.

PEIRCE & FULLER'S
GALLERY OF ART,

MAIN STREET, (opposite Postoffice),

STILLWATER,..............MINNESOTA.

THE PROPRIETORS OF THIS GALLERY are happy to announce to the citizens of Stillwater and adjoining towns, that having recently arrived from the East with

A LARGE AND WELL SELECTED ASSORTMENT OF CASES, FRAMES, ETC.,

They are prepared to give the greatest satisfaction to all those who will give them a call. With a NEW and superior

SKY-LIGHT,

Pictures that speak for themselves, and proprietors who will do all they can to accommodate, they are in hopes of securing the patronage of the public.

AMBROTYPES AND MELAINOTYPES, in double and single cases.

LETTER PICTURES to send to all parts of the world without additional postage.

DAGUERREOTYPES and other pictures copied and warranted BRIGHTER and more durable than the original. Also, pictures taken in Rings, Lockets, Bracelets and Breast Pins.

The public are invited to call and see the rooms and also to inspect the specimens of Art which they are confident cannot be surpassed by any in the State.

E. W. PEIRCE.   B. F. FULLER.

May 21, 1859.   n24tp

An advertisement appearing in the **Stillwater *Democrat*,** May 21, 1859.

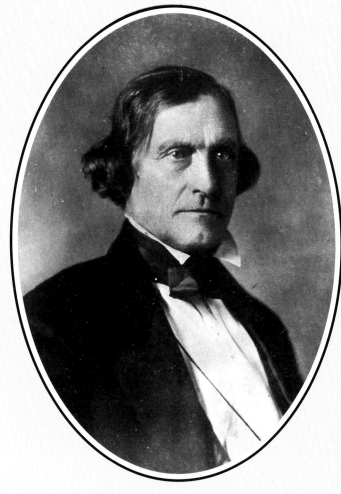

Maj. Joseph R. Brown (1805 - 1870)
ca. 1853.

The original print was a Daguerreotype taken about the time Brown was a newspaper publisher in St. Paul.

JOSEPH Renshaw Brown, the son of the Reverend Samuel Brown of Lancaster, Pennsylvania ran away from a printing apprenticeship at age 14. He joined the 5th Infantry as a fife and drummer boy and arrived at Fort Snelling in 1819. After his military days he explored the territory and reached the Falls of St. Croix by 1837. It is said Brown was the first to float logs down the St. Croix River. Two years later he founded a small trading post at the head of Lake St. Croix naming the post Dakotah. Brown was elected to the Wisconsin territorial legislature and helped create St. Croix County, with his post as the county seat. He was a leading delegate at the Stillwater Convention in 1848, which led to the organization of the Minnesota territory. He served in the territorial house and senate at various times, and in August 1852 Brown purchased St. Paul's newspaper, the *Minnesota Pioneer,* from James M. Goodhue. Five years after purchasing the paper, Brown platted the town of Henderson, Minnesota and started the Henderson *Democrat* newspaper. Joseph Renshaw Brown took an active part in Indian affairs, and was influential during the Dakota uprising of 1862. Brown was also an inventor, and while in New York City perfecting his steam powered tractor, he passed away on November 9, 1870. Joseph Renshaw Brown was a pioneer in the truest sense of the word.

How Stillwater Came to Be

"Here is a little village sprung up like a gourd, but whether it is
to perish as soon, God only knows."
—Rev. W. T. Boutwell

BEFORE settlers could legally expand northwestward into the St. Croix Valley, agreements were needed with the natives who occupied the land. An 1837 treaty with the Chippewa was signed at Fort Snelling, where the Minnesota (St. Peter) River joins the Mississippi. Dated July 29, this treaty ceded all lands of the Chippewa Nation between the Mississippi and St. Croix Rivers with the 46th parallel marking the northern boundary. Governor Dodge of Wisconsin, acting as a commissioner of the United States, spearheaded the act.

In exchange for the tracts of land, the U.S. Government paid the Indian Nation $9,500 in cash, $19,000 in goods, $3,000 for establishing blacksmith shops, $1,000 for farming, $2,000 in provisions, and $500 in tobacco.

Another treaty was signed in Washington, D.C., on September 29, 1837, with the Dakota Nation. By the terms of this treaty, all their lands lying east of the Mississippi River were ceded to the U.S. Government. In payment, the Dakotas received $300,000. Some of the money was divided among the mixed-bloods and more was to be used in payment of their debts.

Upon the ratification of these treaties, white settlers were allowed to explore and settle in the newly-ceded triangle of land between the two rivers. Among these settlers was a soldier, an Indian trader, a promoter, and a politician named Joseph Renshaw Brown. Brown settled a small trading post at the head of Lake St. Croix in 1839. He named the settlement "Dakotah." We now know this area as Schulenberg's Addition to Stillwater, adjacent to the commonly-known group of homes known as "Dutchtown" or "Charlottesburg."

Before 1838, Joseph Brown had never met his half-sister, Lydia, who was living in Illinois with her husband, Paul Carli. Joseph left home at a young age, so the opportunity never arose until he showed up on Lydia's doorstep. Joseph must have been a fairly convincing person because Lydia Carli, her two children and her brother-in-law, Dr. Christopher Carli, made the long and labori-

Lydia A. Carli (1818-1905)
ca. 1887, *John M. Kuhn..*

By taking up house at Dakotah, Lydia became the first white woman in what is now Minnesota. Her story of the first Christmas at Dakotah is legendary. Her first husband, Paul Carli later joined the family and they settled at Lakeland. Paul drowned in Lake St. Croix and Lydia married her brother-in-law Christopher on March 12, 1847. Joseph R. Brown officiated. In later life she insisted that her life story be reported accurately.

Dr. Christopher Carli (1811-1887)
ca. 1885.

Dr. Carli played an important part in the development of early Stillwater. His doctoring and pharmaceutical skills were employed throughout the valley. Carli was educated at Heidelberg University in Germany. He came to the United States in 1832. After another stay in Europe several years later, he practised medicine in Chicago before coming to Dakotah. He opened the first bank in Stillwater and served on the first city council.

ous trip and moved to Dakotah on June 29, 1841. The house built there was known as the Tamarack House: part home, part lodge, part courthouse, part jail.

This move created a couple of firsts. Mrs. Carli became the first white woman in what is now Minnesota, and Dr. Carli, the first practicing physician. In some ways, these facts come into play for Joseph since their presence meant he could go about his business knowing that the house would be kept and that any illnesses and injuries could be treated.

Jacob Fisher, a carpenter and millwright, and Sylvester Statelar, a blacksmith, spent the winter of 1842 at Dakotah. They had met each other at the St. Croix Falls Improvement Company. The following spring, Fisher claimed unsurveyed lands at the head of Lake St. Croix, immediately south of Dakotah. Jake had noticed that the stream running by the trading post was fed by a lake on top of the bluff (McKusick Lake). Further study revealed a large ravine running in the opposite direction of the water flow. With an easy diversion and dam, Fisher determined it could provide enough water power to drive a sawmill.

Seeing this as an employment opportunity, Fisher offered to turn over his claim

John McKusick (1815 - 1900)
ca. 1865.

McKUSICK was born December 18, 1815 in Cornish, Maine. When he was 24 years old, McKusick moved to St. Louis, and the next year moved to St. Croix Falls. There he became interested in logging and when water power was discovered at what is now Stillwater, he and several others came down the St. Croix River and started a lumbermill on October 19, 1843. McKusick was the first to build a frame house in Stillwater, sometime around 1845, and is credited with the naming of the city of Stillwater.

McKusick was married three times. The first time was Miss Phoebe Greeley in 1847; she died soon afterwards. His second wife was Miss Servia Greeley, and the couple had three children: Newton, Chester, and Ella. The second Mrs. McKusick died on February 18, 1887. John McKusick was married a third time to Mrs. Ella Knapp.

When Stillwater was incorporated as a city in 1854, it was John McKusick who was chosen its first mayor. After his term was over, McKusick became Stillwater's second postmaster, succeeding Elam Greeley. McKusick was elected to the Minnesota Senate, serving from 1863 through 1866.

John McKusick was a tall man, about 6 feet, and had a striking personality. He was a supporter of the Ascension church for over fifty years. He passed away quietly in 1900, at the age of 85.

Elam Greeley (1818-1882)
ca. 1852.

Greeley became Stillwater's first postmaster in 1846. He was elected to the Minnesota Territorial Legislature in 1851 and again in 1856. He sold his interest in the first mill to McKusick then consented to logging, rafting and shipping until his accidental death at Cumberland, Wisconsin on September 15, 1882.

to Elias McKean and Calvin F. Leach if they would build a mill on the land. At that time there were only two other mills on the St. Croix, one at the falls (St. Croix Falls) and one at Marine Mills, the first business in what is now Minnesota.

At that time, John McKusick and Elam Greeley were passing through and stopped off at the Tamarack House. They were looking for a good site to build a sawmill and soon learned of Fisher's offer. After some negotiations the four men agreed to build on Fisher's claim. McKusick went to St. Louis for machinery and provisions. On his return in October, the company was formed—the Stillwater Lumber Company. A few years later, John McKusick became the sole owner.

A crew of about a dozen men already had built a series of shacks and shanties, and over the winter they worked on the mill itself.

By April 1, 1844, the mill was finished and operated a short time until the spring floods. This was the first frame building erected in Stillwater, and was located east of Main Street, on lot 8, block 18. The second building was McKusick's boarding house, up the hill from the mill on what became Myrtle Street. McKusick also built a company store at what is now the corner of Myrtle and Main streets. Sylvester Statelar set up a blacksmith shop nearby.

As word spread of the new mill, settlers began arriving. The John Allen family was the first to settle in the new village, followed by Anson Northrup's family. Northrup, whose claim covered everything south of Chestnut Street, built a hotel south of the mill only to sell the building in the fall to William Willim. Another Northrup House was built between his original hotel and the mill. Northrup later built famous hotels in other parts of the state.

A missionary, the Rev. William T. Boutwell, arrived in the mill town, gathering the flock at McKusick's boarding house. He preached the first sermon within the new village that first summer. Boutwell would permanently locate in Stillwater by 1847, holding regular services in the Northrup House dining hall.

Socrates Nelson set up a general store near the Northrup House. Saloons soon became part of the main street fare. A crude, but entertaining bowling lane is said to have been installed at this time.

As the prosperity spread and more work was created, the workers sent for their families. By 1846, only two years after the Stillwater mill began, at least 10 married couples made "Stillwater" their home.

THE Reverend Boutwell was graduated from Dartmouth College in 1828, then from Andover Theological Seminary three years later. On June 13, 1831, he left for Mackinaw (Michigan) with the expectation of establishing missions among the Chippewa Indians. Skilled in the language of the Chippewa, the Rev. Boutwell was invited by Henry Schoolcraft to tour the Northwest and explore the territory to find sites for new mission stations. The tour started at Fond du Lac, proceeded up the St. Louis River and portaged to the Mississippi. From there they paddled upstream and reached Leech Lake and further on Cass Lake, the reputed source of the Mississippi. However, the expedition learned that Cass Lake was not the true source, and so they continued on. They found themselves in another lake, in which Schoolcraft asked Boutwell for a Latin word for true source. Boutwell could only think of "veritas caput," meaning true head. Schoolcraft then took the second and third syllables of the first word and the first syllable of the second and combined them to form the name of the lake—Itasca.

Rev. William Boutwell (1803-1890)
ca. 1888, *John M. Kuhn..*

Lt. Governor William Holcombe (1804-1870)
ca. 1859.

Holcombe was a member of both the Wisconsin and Minnesota constitutional conventions, serving at both on the finance committee. He attended the territorial convention at Stillwater on August 26, 1848, and was elected the state's first lieutenant governor in 1858. Holcombe died while serving his second term as Stillwater's mayor.

The first post office was established that year with Elam Greeley being the postmaster.

By 1848, the Stillwater community was one of the fastest growing in the territory. St. Paul and St. Anthony saw Stillwater as a threat to their growth. Many individuals thought Stillwater was destined to be the largest city in the region.

Sarah Louise Judd, the first school teacher, married future book store owner Ariel Eldridge. She was the first in the region to make Daguerreotypes, the early photography process named after the Frenchman Louis Daguerre. To have a photographer in Stillwater was impressive. There was no other photographer for hundreds of miles. Her work spanned several years. None of her photographs is thought to exist today.

Other photographers in Stillwater during the late 1850s and 1860s were C. E. Chetlain and B. Truaisch, E. W. Peirce and B. F. Fuller, and E. F. Everitt. During the 1860s and 1870s, James Sinclair, J. A. Stridborg, Chris Carli Jr. and Frank E. Loomis were the prominent photographers.

During the 1840s, there was no order among the loggers and mills. The traffic and logs on the river were haphazard, but with only a few mills, everything seemed to even out. However, as the number of logs increased and with mills mushrooming up and down the St. Croix and Mississippi, the disarray multiplied, leading to many disorderly situations.

To put some order into the industry, the principal loggers elected William Holcombe as the first surveyor general, the government official who oversaw lumbering activities on the river, settling disputes, counting board feet of lumber, and registering log marks. Holcombe later served as the state's first lieutenant governor.

It was surmised that 11 million feet of cut logs had passed through in 1848, an unconscionable amount for that time; but once steam mills were put into operation in the 1850s, the number increased 27 fold in twenty years.

On September 12, 1848, the Village of Stillwater, Wisconsin Territory was officially surveyed and platted by Harvey Wilson. The shoreline of Lake St. Croix at Stillwater is clearly marked. It is much different today. Main Street was only a few blocks long with the original Stillwater mill at the north end and the bluff to the south. Other streets, many not completed for another 30 to 40 years, were platted for the first time. Other streets were never completed or abandoned due to impassible conditions.

On May 29, 1848, Wisconsin became the 30th state of the Union. With Wisconsin's western boundary located at the St. Croix River, anything west of that was left out, unorganized, without any government control. To solve this, a convention was called at Stillwater on August 26, 1848. On that date, 61 delegates from the unorganized territory assembled at 10 A.M. and elected the following officers: M.S. Wilkerson, president; David S. Lambert, secretary.

The convention laid out the new territory and named the area "Minnesota," a Dakota word suggested by Joseph R. Brown which means "sky-tinted waters." Resolutions were drafted to be delivered to Washington, D.C., and presented by a delegate elected at the convention. This delegate was Henry Hastings Sibley, who worked for the American Fur Company at Mendota, and would later become Minnesota's first state governor.

On March 3, 1849, through the efforts of the Stillwater Convention, an act of Congress formed the new territory of Minnesota.

The new territory set up its government with the first chief justice of the territorial Supreme Court Aaron Goodrich appointed by President Zachary Taylor on March 19, 1849. Court began in Stillwater on August 13, 1849, with thirty-five cases on the docket heard over six days. The first murder trial under territorial law also took place in Stillwater in February 1850. In that case, a thirteen-year-old boy named Snow had been killed by a boy about the same age. The boy was found guilty of manslaughter and was sentenced to ninety days in the guardhouse at Fort Snelling.

After the organization of the territory, the river village of Stillwater kept expanding. In 1850, A. M. Crosby opened a gunsmith shop; R. Hussey began a bakery, Norbert Kimmick started a brewery in his kitchen, and the first circus, a visit of the Antonio Brothers, spread its tent in Stillwater that summer.

On January 16, 1851, a bill was introduced to the territorial Legislature to locate the capital at St. Paul and the prison at Stillwater. It passed on February 7, 1851, and was signed into law the same day by Alexander Ramsey, the territorial governor. Both buildings were completed in 1853.

On the night of May 13, 1852, after more than a month of heavy rain, McKusick's lake overflowed its banks and a tremendous amount of dirt, sand, mud, and silt came rushing down the heavily-deforested hills above Stillwater. Five to eight acres of downtown land was affected. Several feet of mud filled the stores and homes around Main Street, which already was subjected to regular periods of high water. Past Main Street the mudslide filled in the bogs and marsh along the shore.

When the mud dried, what was once nearly worthless land from Second Street to the river was transformed into excellent commercial property. The price per acre shot up from $1.25 to almost $500. What was supposed to be a disaster for McKusick turned out to be a blessing in disguise.

Stillwater was incorporated as a city in the Minnesota territory on March 4, 1854, the same day as St. Paul.

The local citizenry fittingly chose as mayor the man who founded the city and who also is credited with choosing the name of Stillwater, John McKusick.

James S. Norris and Samuel Register were elected to represent the area in the territorial Legislature.

As Stillwater was settling in as a town, a newcomer was settling in with his family. This man, Isaac Staples, would soon become an important lumberman and civic leader, shaping the future of the new city.

St. Croix Steam Gang Saw Mills, North Main Street, Isaac Staples, proprietor. ca. 1870. *Northwestern View Company,* Lyons, Iowa.
Publicity photographs like this one were distributed in the days prior to high quality newspaper and magazine advertisements.

Industry & Commerce 2

"Do you still ask what is Stillwater? It is the natural receptacle of the countless millions of logs that for a long time to come will float down the river St. Croix. Stillwater will be a second Bangor [Maine] in the lumber trade. Nothing can prevent it."

—St. Croix Union, *May 26, 1855*

WHAT John McKusick and others had started in 1843 was not just another river town in the expanding Northwest, but also its primary industry of the next seventy years. The McKusick mill, actually the third lumber mill on the St. Croix River, was quickly followed by others. In 1850, Sawyer and Heaton constructed a mill in Stillwater (Main and Laurel Streets), and in 1854 two more were built, one by Isaac Staples and Samuel F. Hersey, the other by Schulenberg, Boeckeler & Company, near Brown's old settlement of Dakotah.

To help organize the logs coming down the river, the territorial legislature organized the St. Croix Boom Company on February 7, 1851. The incorporators were: Orange Walker and George B. Judd, of Marine Mills, Minnesota; John McKusick, Socrates Nelson, and Levi Churchill, of Stillwater, Minnesota; Daniel Mears and William Kent, of Osceola, Wisconsin; and W. H. C. Folsom, of Taylor's Falls, Minnesota.

The first boom, which is an area to count and sort the millions of logs floating down river, was placed just above Osceola, WI. After several reorganizations, the boom was moved to one and one-half mile above Stillwater, Minnesota. As more territory was logged, the river began to get crowded. From only 8.5 million feet in 1843-44 to the peak of more than 450 million feet of logs in 1890, someone had to oversee the industry and that became the job of the surveyor of logs. The first surveyor was William Holcombe. Others that followed included: Zenas W. Chase, John S. Proctor, A. C. Hospes, Jacob Bean (1889-1894), B. J. Mosier (1899-1900), and J. G. Armson (1905-1908)

Isaac Staples arrived in Stillwater and built a lumber mill in 1854 near Kimmick's brewery south of downtown. This was the start of one of the largest lumber dynasties in the upper Midwest. He built this first mill with a partner named Samuel F. Hersey, of Maine. Staples engaged in a number of businesses with partners until 1869, when, upon mutual consent, a general division occurred and Staples handled his interests

Office scene at Hersey & Bean Lumber Co., 735 South Main Street. ca. 1890.
Second from left, bookkeeper George L. Patchin; middle, Addie Matthews.
Printed on the reverse of this photo and its mate opposite: "This photograph was made with a Kodak Camera. T. W. Ingersoll, agency for the Kodak. St. Paul, Minnesota." The original Kodak, George Eastman's first amateur box camera using flexible film, was patented in September 1888.

by himself. He built or bought other mills and was largely engaged in the logging business until his death in 1898.

Staples' first mill, built in 1854, was sold to Hersey, Bean, & Brown. George Henry Atwood came to Stillwater in 1884 and worked for the firm in the office. Two years later he was an officer of the company. By November 1891 Atwood found himself financially stable enough to lease the entire mill under his own name. Atwood then purchased the Schulenberg-Boeckeler mill in 1901, and it was then called the Atwood "B" mill. George Atwood was the first of the valley lumbermen to haul in lumber by railroad, beginning in 1894. Atwood's "A" mill operated until 1904, and his "B" mill was destroyed by fire.

Atwood began the Twin City Forge and Foundry Company just before the first World War. During that conflict, the company produced munitions to help the war effort. Atwood was partners with Frederick Weyerhaueser and William Sauntry in the Atwood Lumber Company in Willow River, Minnesota.

William Sauntry came to Stillwater and worked with Albert Tozer, the firm name being Sauntry & Tozer. When Tozer retired, Sauntry purchased his share and engaged in business alone. Sauntry leased the stock of the St. Croix Boom Company from the heirs of Martin Mower, and Sauntry built the Nevers dam several miles above Taylor's Falls, Minnesota, which was run under his management for many years. He had interests in other companies such as The Ann River Land Company, Rutledge Lumber and Manufacturing Company, and the Pine Tree Lumber Company. At one time, Sauntry's wealth was estimated at over two million dollars. However, with poor advice and bad investments, his fortune dwindled. With these events, Sauntry committed suicide in the Hotel Ryan in St. Paul, Minnesota on November 10, 1914.

With the depletion of the forest land in the area, the lumber industry suffered so that in 1914, the same year William Sauntry took his life, the last log passed through the St. Croix Boom. This marked the end of Stillwater's sawmilling era, the industry that created the city.

The lumber industry helped spawn other industries in the river community. With the abundance of wood, many related companies took root in Stillwater. Furniture companies started because of the vast array of lumber. The first, opened by Thomas Lowery in 1854, was sold two years later to

Atwood's office at Hersey & Bean Lumber Co., 735 South Main Street. ca. 1890.
Pictured (L-R) are company bookkeeper James H. McGarry and secretary George H. Atwood. When Atwood bought the mill a few years later, McGarry stayed on. By 1900, Atwood's name would be found in the names of three different companies: Atwood Lumber Co. (Frederick Weyerhaueser, president), Atwood & Bean, and Atwood & Jones Manufacturing Co., a box manufacturing business.

Three Davids. ca. 1902, *Emil Okerblad.*
**David Swain (1841-1918), David Tozer (1823-1905)
and David Carmichael (1835-1908) got together for
this "Three Davids" photograph. Swain was a
boatmaker, Tozer was in the land and log
business, and Carmichael was in the lumber
business. These three industries were all keenly
tied together.**

Stillwater's business leaders at the turn of the century were not of the same standing as a Rockefeller or Carnegie, but the money flowing from wood-related industries was still quite evident. Take, for instance, the men who were on the board of directors of the various financial institutions in 1900. They included: James Mulvey (logs), Samuel McClure (logs), E. L. Hospes (lumber), David Bronson (logs and steamboats), Roscoe F. Hersey (land and logs), David Tozer (logs), William Sauntry (land, logs and manufacturing), Elmore Lowell (hotel), Edwin D. Buffington (manufacturing), Austin T. Jenks (wholesale grocer), William Chalmers (lumber).

Compare that with today's main industries and one will find that manufacturing, hotels and groceries continue, but the logs and lumber industry has moved elsewhere.

Around the time that lumbering was fading as an industry in the St. Croix Valley, business leaders began to move with the industry.

Stillwater newspapers in the 1910s were promoting Stillwater as an excellent place to locate a business. Full-page advertisements were taken out to promote the local business climate which had suffered a major decline.

"Shop at home" was a calling cry throughout the 1930s and 1940s. Retail businesses were in the decline as locals were able to easily drive to St. Paul to shop.

By the early 1970s, downtown Stillwater was a far-cry from the days of the 1890s. Many of the older buildings were torn down or heavily remodeled to match that of recent shopping centers.

William Sauntry (1853-1914)
ca. 1890, *Laurentz Wicklund.*

Calvin M. Hathaway (1828-1894) began blacksmithing and horseshoeing in 1855 on Main Street. Son William H. Hathaway helped move the business up to 3rd Street in 1880. In digging the hill for the building, a spring yielding 700 barrels of water a day was discovered. The Hathaways put in a 300 barrel reservoir and diversified into the spring water business as well as the awning business. His brother Harry L. Hathaway (1869-1935) joined him as Hathaway Brothers in the 1890s, but William moved on to Montana leaving Harry in charge. It's believed that Harry is the man holding the bridle and daughter Lillian is nearby.

M. S. Willard whom later sold it in 1880 to J. Fowler, Jr. Another one, the Simonet Furniture Company, is still in business today.

Sebastian Simonet arrived in Stillwater in 1864 and started a cabinet business, making his own wares. He soon started having such demand that he would carry other manufacturer's furniture. After his death in 1886, the business was carried on by his sons Ludwig, Felix, and for a short time, Aloyisus. In 1904, the Simonet Furniture Company purchased the site of the burned Grand Opera House, the site they still occupy today. The third generation of Simonets took over the business until 1971 when the fourth generation stepped in, soon joined by a fifth generation. They are: Jim O'Brien, Joe O'Brien, Joe (Dode) Simonet, Paul Simonet, Brian Simonet, Colleen O'Brien Kruse and Tom O'Brien.

The Simonet Furniture Company is the oldest furniture store in Minnesota and thought to be the oldest family owned furniture business in the United States.

Another company that was a by-product of the lumber industry was Seymour, Sabin & Company. This company was located across from the state prison on North Main Street and used prison labor to help produce one of the biggest-selling threshing machines in the country, the "Minnesota Chief." The company also manufactured doors, sash, cooperage, general office fixtures, etc.

During Stillwater's early years, local news was mainly spread by word of mouth. With the increasing population, other ways to pass along news were needed. So on October 23, 1854, Stillwater's first newspaper hit the streets. It was called the *St. Croix Union,* and lasted only three years. However, the *Union* set the standard for future newspapers that followed.

The next paper, the Stillwater *Messenger,* was first issued on September 11, 1856, edited by A. J. Van Vorhes. A. B. Easton, after working with the *Messenger* for several years, started the Stillwater *Gazette* on August 6, 1870. The *Gazette,* at first a weekly newspaper, began a daily edition on August 25, 1884 and continues that pace today. The Easton family owned and edited the *Gazette* for over one hundred years until it was sold by John Easton, the fifth generation, in 1987. However, the first daily newspaper in Stillwater was the *Daily Sun,* which lasted from 1881 through 1884. Its weekly version was known as the *Lumberman.* One other daily paper that made an appearance for a brief time in 1890 was called the *Daily Call.*

Ed O'Brien Sample Rooms, Excelsior Block, North Main Street. ca. 1895.

The Ed O'Brien Sample Rooms opened in the Excelsior Block in 1882. The grand opening was a real smash, especially when one of the patrons tried unsuccessfully to walk through one of the French plate glass windows. In this photo, the windows reveal some interesting scenes across the street.

A S soon as McKusick's mill was completed in 1843, he proceeded to construct a boarding house nearby that would house the mill workers. The following year, 1844, Anson Northrup built the Northrup House, the first full-fledged hotel in Stillwater.

This hotel burned in December 1847 then rebuilt the following year and given the name of the St. Croix House. This hotel was later destroyed by fire in 1877.

The Minnesota House was to be a private residence for Elam Greeley in 1846, however, Greeley sold the house to Judd & Walker before it was completed. They finished the house and turned it into a hotel. In 1849, the Lake House was built by John H. Brewster, and the house was destroyed in 1874 by fire. Other early Stillwater hotels included the

TOP: Main and Chestnut Streets, showing St. Croix House and Min[n]esota House. April 1865, *E. F. Everett.*
Notice that the word Minnesota on the sign is missing an "n." As talk of calling the territory "Minesota" heightened, the sign painter used the single "n" spelling before the 1848 territorial convention had adopted the two "n" spelling. This hotel passed out of the rooming business in the 1870s and was torn down in 1881 to make room for the Tepass block. On the left, the St. Croix House is seen set back from the street. Later photos suggest the building was moved up to the boardwalk.

RIGHT: The Sawyer House, 2nd & Myrtle Streets. ca. 1871, *James Sinclair*
The Sawyer House proved to be more than just a boarding house. It was the convention center of its day. Many important meetings and gatherings took place in the house during its many years. This print has been altered to cover up barrels and crates stored along the south side of the building.

The Lowell Inn, Myrtle and 2nd Streets, August 1992, *Dean R. Thilgen.*

Rivertown Inn, 306 West Olive Street. 1991, *Chuck Dougherty*
What's old is new again. The bed and breakfast scene in Stillwater began here with the O'Brien house. Now known as the Rivertown Inn, it mixes the older, classic home atmosphere with modern comforts.

Stillwater House, built in 1869 by Peter Alderman; The Williams House, built in 1870; in October 1870, Frank Raiter built the Wexio Hotel; The Keystone House was built in 1872 by Horace Voligny; and the Central House was built by August Booren in the spring of 1879.

In 1857, Henry Sawyer built the Sawyer House on Second Street. It was managed by A. B. Whitcher until 1862, when Albert and Jacob Lowell took over. In 1864, the hotel was sold to Isaac Staples who two years later sold it to Dudley Hall, who owned it until 1871. The Lowells leased the house from Hall until 1871, when Albert Lowell bought the Sawyer House outright. The Sawyer House served the Stillwater area until it was torn down in 1924 and replaced in 1927 by the Lowell Inn. In 1930, the Inn was purchased by Arthur and Nell Palmer, and is still is managed by Arthur and Maureen Palmer and their children Mary (Palmer) Simon and Steve Palmer. The Lowell Inn still stands as an ornament to the city.

In the 1970s and 1980s, a transformation in the inn business was taking place throughout the Midwest. The city's big, beautiful homes were either being torn down to make way for apartment complexes or the homes themselves were being cut up into three, four, or more units, thus destroying their rich history and heritage. In 1982, Sherwood and Gloria Van Gaard took the John O'Brien mansion at 306 West Olive Street and turned it into the first Bed and Breakfast in Stillwater (and the second licensed Bed and Breakfast in Minnesota). It is called the Rivertown Inn (now owned by Chuck and Judy Dougherty). As a "B & B," the owners maintain the home more as it was originally built while affording the large cost of living in such a house. The bed and breakfast idea became so popular that by 1991, the William Sauntry Mansion, the Heirloom Inn, the Battle Hollow B & B, and most recently, the Ann Bean B & B, the Brunswick Inn, the James Mulvey Inn, and the Elephant Walk had joined the Rivertown in this unique venture.

OPPOSITE: Bronson & Folsom display at a street fair, Chestnut and Main Streets. ca. 1899.
Held for a few years around the turn of the century, Stillwater street fairs were the equivalent of today's county fair. Exhibits, parades, booths and peddlers dominated Main Street for a few days. Local businesses would set up a booth with a particular theme. Bronson and Folsom set up a fruit and vegetable display. Bronson and Folsom grocery was one of Stillwater's longest-running businesses.

Since these early attempts, many other newspapers have come and gone in Stillwater, such as *Der Hermann Sohn Im Westen,* a German newspaper; *Vesterlandet,* a Scandinavian paper; *The Washington County Post; The Washington County Journal; The Trade News; and The Post-Messenger.*

Today there are three newspapers that focus their coverage on Stillwater and the surrounding area: The Stillwater *Gazette, The Courier News,* and the *St. Croix Valley Press.*

With the big, husky lumbermen coming back to town after a hard winter in the woods, many of them would take time to amble down to the local saloon to wet their whistles and tell tall tales. The first such establishment in Stillwater was started by John Morgan in 1848. He was followed by Berry & Farmer, and many others. In 1881, there were 27 saloons in Stillwater; in 1884 there were 57 drinking establishments in the river city. Today, such places include John's Bar (established in 1922), the Mad Capper Saloon & Eatery, Cat Ballou's, Trump's Deluxe Bar & Grill, Canelake's St. Croix Club, Meister's Bar & Grill on the South Hill (since 1898), and several others.

To make it a little easier to get the supply needed to sell to the hardy lumbermen, breweries quickly followed. In 1851, Norbert Kimmick started a small whiskey still on the corner of Third and Chestnut Streets. It was located in his kitchen and produced about five barrels a week. In 1852, Kimmick built a brewery south of downtown, and in 1854 he formed a partnership with Frank Aiple. With Kimmick's death in 1857, his widow Susanna operated the brewery until January 2, 1860 when she married Aiple. The brewery burned in May 1868. A new building was being built when Aiple died on November 5, 1868. Again, Susanna Aiple had to run the operation until again she married in December 1869, to Herman Tepass.

About this same time Martin Wolf started a brewery at the corner of Main and Nelson Streets in the spring of 1868. In March 1871, the brewery became known as the Wolf, Tanner and Company. Not long after, a devastating fire at the brewery killed two men. Wolf's brewery was immediately rebuilt.

In May 1876, Joseph Wolf purchased the entire company renaming it the Joseph Wolf Company—Empire Brewery.

IN 1882, Byron Mosier took a partner into his business. This partner from Chicago, stood 7 feet 9 inches tall, weighed about 350 pounds, was a Native American and carried a tomahawk in his right hand. This "silent partner" stood on a cigar crate outside Mosier's Cigar Store at Main and Chestnut Streets for over forty years and frightened many drunken lumberjacks. This was the Mosier Cigar Store Indian.

The Indian was carved from two pieces of pine, one piece formed the entire body and head of the statue, and the other piece formed the right arm and tomahawk. On the crate on which the Indian stood, there was an inscription which read: "I greet you for the tribe to the 'Friendly Valley.' That's my job since 1882." The only time that the Indian left his post was when floodwaters would wash him down river.

When Mosier's store closed, the Indian was purchased by Mr. and Mrs. Arthur Palmer and was displayed at the north end of the Lowell Inn's veranda, around 1934. In October 1939, the Indian was loaned to the Century Celebration Decoration Committee in Minneapolis and was put on display for one week at the Young & Quinlan store.

In 1940, the Indian was sold to a person who gave it to the Dayton's department store founder as a present. It was displayed in Southdale shopping center beginning in 1950. The Indian spent some time in Donald Dayton's garden. In October 1969, Donald Dayton donated the Mosier Cigar Store Indian to the Minnesota Historical Society, where it can be found stored in a crate.

In 1980, some people in the valley started looking for the Indian. An article in the Fall/Winter issue of the publication called The *Fishwrapper* started the search, asking for information from the public. It wasn't until 1985 that the Washington County Historical Society located it at the state historical society.

The next year, 1986, the Washington County Historical Society obtained the Indian on loan from the state and displayed it over the summer and fall at the Warden's House Museum in Stillwater. The Indian was then returned to the state historical society, against the will of some of the residents in Stillwater.

Many people still believe that the cigar store Indian belongs in Stillwater, and that the Minnesota Historical Society should give or loan the Indian back to the people of Stillwater. Now that the state History Center has three large exhibit areas, the Mosier Tobacco Store Indian may one day find a spot in one.

The lumbermen were a bunch of men who worked hard, but they were also family men and this meant they, at one time or another, would need new suits of clothes and shoes.

Kolliner Bros. & Newman Company, manufacturers of fine clothing, was organized in 1904 with Max M. Kolliner as president and Phillip Newman as vice president. Kolliner's Menswear continues in the city, at 119 South Main Street.

J. O'Shaughnessy began making boots and shoes in Stillwater in 1862, with many others to follow. August Buth started in 1870 on Chestnut Street; Nicholas F. Schwarz began in 1873; P. J. Stenstrom made boots and shoes in 1874; The Ferguson Brothers started on March 18, 1878. However, the most common name for shoes and boots in Stillwater was the Connolly Shoe Company which began production in 1905. Connolly's shoes sold nationally until cheaper foreign shoes began to become common, putting the local shoemaker out of business in the late 1960s. Towards the end of their business, the shoe company introduced kangaroo hide shoes. When the factory shut down the left over stock was sold, creating a new retail business, the Connco shoe company. They were

in business for about 20 years and had stores around the region. The stores were sold-out to the now-defunct Crown Shoes chain.

For a farmer and lumberman alike, the barber shop provided a few comforts not found at home. The busiest time of the week was Saturday night, most shops staying open until midnight. It was common to get a hot bath for 25¢. Doing so on a Saturday would properly prepare one for the Sabbath.

Some of the prominent early barbers in town were Sam Hadley, Charley Jackson, Luke Doyle, and the O. K. Barber shop run by George Rogentine and Bartholomew McSweeney. By 1880, everything was not OK, and Rogentine left to start his own shop.

It should go without saying that the lumberjacks were hardy eaters, and that was true with the rest of Stillwater. In 1860 Joseph Dahm's grocery store was built on lower Main Street beneath the bluff. Bronson-Folsom grocery actually began in the fall of 1865. These two, along with David Cover, started the firm Bronson, Cover & Company. This firm went out of business in 1871, and immediately David Bronson and E. A. Folsom joined together to form Bronson-Folsom. A couple years later, the two took on two others and

formed Hersey, Bronson, Doe & Folsom. This firm lasted only a few years, when the firm again became Bronson-Folsom.

Meat markets were, and still are, popular in Stillwater. Dennis J. Hooley opened a meat market on the South Hill in 1876. Hooley eventually moved into the grocery business in downtown Stillwater. In the third generation of the family business, Jack and Charlie Hooley began in 1968 what they called Consumers United for Buying known today as CUB Foods. CUB Foods was purchased by the Super Value food store chain in 1980. There are now 89 CUB Food stores in thirteen states. Super Value plans to continue the Hooley tradition by building a new supermarket at Main and Myrtle Streets, the block where Stillwater began 150 years ago.

The Kilty Brothers opened a meat and grocery business in March 1878. George Giebler, who started working for D. J. Hooley as a meat cutter, opened his own meat market, called the Union Meat Market in the Union Block of downtown Stillwater.

Another family meat market was called Brine's Meats, which was started in 1958 by Lamont "Bud" Brine. Brine bought the meat market from the Hanson family at 210 South Main Street. In 1974, Brine's moved to 219 South Main, the old Stillwater Hardware Store. In 1976, Brine's opened their Employee Lunch Room on the second floor. The business was so popular that in 1981 Brine's opened another deli and restaurant in St. Paul. Tragically a fire in the Stillwater store meant a major remodeling, but business remained good. The meat market outgrew downtown Stillwater and so a new retail store on the southwest edge of town was built. The downtown bar and restaurant and St. Paul establishment continue to delight its customers.

Typical of many other towns, Stillwater's industrial and retail development is traced back to lumbering. Looking back over one-hundred fifty years, one can follow how the various trades developed and flourished. As the lumber disappeared, however, so did the economy of the valley. Today the area is just as dependent on the lumber industry, not for wood products, but for the heritage and the history it continues to carry in new industries. These include antique stores, dinner train rides, bed and breakfasts, history museums, and the lumberjack festival that is celebrated in Stillwater. The burly lumbermen still help Stillwater's economy. 🪵

Giebler Bros. Meats, Union block, 310 South Main Street. January 1921.

Nels Hanson ran a meat market at 308 South Main ever since the Union Block was built about 1875. George and Charles Giebler took over about 1903 and called it the Union Meat Market. Today we find this spot occupied by Tremblay's Sweet Shop. Around 1911 John Giebler moved down a couple doors to 312 South Main Street. And later still, about 1917, Giebler Brothers opened next door at 310 South Main. John died about 1936 and brother George kept the market going with Henry S. Berglund until about 1944.

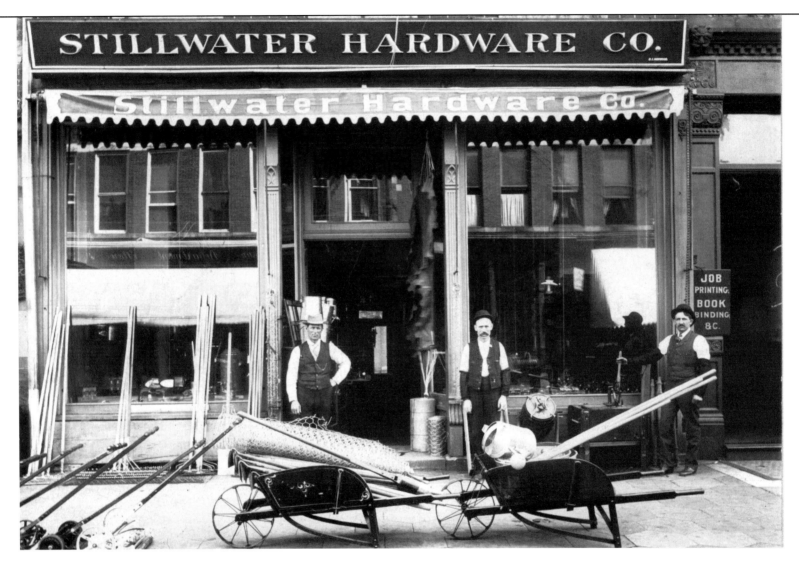

Stillwater Hardware Co., 219 South Main Street. ca. 1898.
Clerks Nick Backe (1859-1936), James Heffernan Jr. (1858-1929), and Oscar Garbush (1875-1926). In 1974 Brine's Meat Market moved into this location.

Barber shop, 230 South Main Street. ca. 1900.

(L-R) John A. F. Krueger (1867-1913), William Patterson (1868-1949), Patrick Garrity (1855-1935). In those days, tonsorial skills included simple surgeries and medicinal treatments. One also needed to be skilled at using a straight razor. Rows of shaving mugs can be seen behind Garrity. Customers kept their own mugs right at the shop. Hot or cold baths cost only 25¢. These guys were the forerunners to Smitty, Foxy's and Jim.

STILLWATER'S citizens waited many years before railroad service began. In 1856 a route from Stillwater to St. Paul was authorized, but the Civil War passed and still no tracks had been laid. Instead, the railroad expanded west from St. Paul with no survey even being attempted to Stillwater.

Former mayor, town founder, and businessman John McKusick and twelve other businessmen of the area weren't going to wait for Easterners to build to Stillwater. So in 1867 they formed the Stillwater and St. Paul railroad. This 18-mile line was in reality a branch of the larger Lake Superior and Mississippi railroad which was being laid from St. Paul to Duluth.

This branch, which started at White Bear, was completed to Schulenburg's Addition on December 29, 1870. This new connection to the outside world changed everyone's lives. Immediately the mails were shifted from the daily stage to the train. Shipments of goods of all kinds to and from Stillwater could occur year-round, not just when boats could travel. The route was fairly direct to St. Paul and Minneapolis, whereas the river route went by way of Point Douglas.

The first depot was a very simple structure. Completed that first winter, it was moved to Myrtle Street when the tracks were completed the next summer. A second, more lasting depot was built there as well.

A second railroad had begun its route to Stillwater from St. Paul that same year. This was the St. Paul, Stillwater and Taylor's Falls railroad although it never made it past Stillwater, and its line is better known for connecting up at Hudson. The general manager was a former Stillwater teacher, attorney, newspaper editor, and school superintendent, Alpheus B. Stickney. He later went on to build the Chicago Great Western road.

The old Butler warehouse on South Main was converted into a depot. It lasted until the Chicago, St. Paul, Minneapolis and Omaha railroad was formed in 1881 when it was replaced with a standard passenger and freight depot. It too, was replaced about ten years later with a brick structure that stood for another eighty years.

A third railroad entered Stillwater in 1882, a branch of the St. Paul and Milwaukee. It ran along the west bank of the St. Croix from Hastings to Stillwater. A substantial depot was opened January 1, 1883 that still stands today.

Being at the end of the line of four branches under three railroads complicated Stillwater's rail service. Each railroad had its own depot, a situation which was cause enough for the locals to sign a petition calling for a union passenger depot. The transfer company which linked the railroads together took on the depot project. This company was one of the many concerns of Sen. Dwight M. Sabin.

However, Sen. Sabin's financial empire began to unravel in 1884. Although under receivership the transfer company went ahead with construction in July 1887. The depot architects were Edward Burling and Francis M. Whitehouse of Chicago. The builder of the Grand Opera House, L. W. Eldred, was again the contractor for the union depot.

Morris D. Crotto (1904-1969) and his mother Martha behind the counter at the Depot Cafe, Union Depot, Water and Myrtle Streets. Summer 1939.
Morrie's entire family worked at the cafe at one time or another: his mother, father David, brother Lloyd, sister-in-law Geraldine, wife Ruby and daughter Joanne Weiss Zang. Crotto's specialty was roast beef sandwiches. Saturday night was the busiest and baked beans and ham was popular.

Joseph Carroll (1873-1979)
October 16, 1954, *St. Paul Pioneer Press.*

Standing near the Union Depot clock tower, Joe Carroll smiles for the newspaper photographer while inside the ticket office prepares to close up shop one last time. Opened in January 1888, the last day came October 16, 1954. A few months later the depot was owned by UFE.

Opened with a gala charity ball in January 1888, an injunction kept trains away for the first couple weeks. As well, the transfer company which included the depot went on the auction block and was sold for $100,000. A new transfer company tried but failed as well. A third transfer company lasted until 1902.

James J. Hill, the Empire Builder, gave his approval to the Northern Pacific railway to purchase the transfer company. After a number of good years, once the lumber business dried up and automobiles were becoming commonplace, the NP ceased running passenger service to the depot in September 1927. The other rail companies cut back as well.

Many different businesses operated out of the old Union Station as it was formally called. At the opening of the depot, a fancy restaurant was located on the second floor and a barber shop run by Sam Hadley was on the first. A newspaper stand under the auspices of Malcom McPherson was located there for a long time. The Northern Pacific kept open a ticket office there until October 1954 despite not having passenger service for 27 years! The St. Croix Post located its printing equipment in the back room for a number of years. The mens' waiting room had a lunch counter that was revived in April 1931. Operated by longtime Stillwater cook Thomas McAloon, Morey Crotto took over the restaurant in June 1932 calling it the Depot Cafe, which continued until the building was sold in 1955. He subsequently relocated to North Main Street and moved to the Excelsior Block in 1962.

In 1946 at the request of the Stillwater Association, the womens' waiting room was converted into the bus depot. However, being open at odd hours without close supervision lent to vandalism of the bathrooms. Morey was forced to chase out many hoodlums that were attracted to the old building.

By 1952, the bus depot had closed, and the room was used as a painting studio for the St. Croix Valley Art Group until 1955. In the back rooms a new concern, United Fabricators and Electronics and its owner Russell Gilbert were making radio and television parts. He subsequently bought the old depot and took ownership February 1, 1955. He stayed until a new building was built on South Greeley in 1959.

Originally the Stillwater *Gazette* and Minneapolis *Star* reported that the old depot was to be saved, used as offices by Hooley's. But instead, the adjacent Lumberman's Exchange, an office building built by the old transfer company was saved.

The old depot was demolished during February and March 1960. 🚂

Union Depot in action, Water and Myrtle Streets. September 14, 1926, *John Runk Jr.*

Northern Pacific engine #457, a class D-3 4-6-0 is nearing the end of its life. When NP passenger service ends one year later, the old relic gets sent to the scrap heap. She was built by Baldwin about 1890 for light freight and passenger use. The Milwaukee and Omaha roads continued limited mixed service until the mid-1950s.

Stagecoach and stores at 305, 315 & 319 South Main Street, ca. 1890.

The railroads had eliminated many runs, but a daily "stage" to Marine was still being run. The Main Street stores shown here are J. O. Holen grocery located in the Opera House block, William Kennemann Sons hardware, and Simonet Brothers furniture. After the 1902 Opera House fire, Simonet's moved into that location.

Water wagon, Water Street. ca. 1910.

Patrick Hurley (1860-1950) sitting atop his water wagon in downtown Stillwater. For over 50 years Hurley sprinkled the city's dirt streets to keep the dust down and also filled the cisterns for local customers. Hurley also owned a gravel pit in Oak Park.

John Runk, Jr. (1878-1964), photographer, 110 South Main Street. 1915, *John Runk Jr.*
A Runk self-portrait. Runk was not your typical portrait photographer. He copied old photos for a special historical collection, climbed poles to get the perfect shot of a building on fire, invented record-player cleaning devices, and set up award-winning window displays. It's no wonder he was in business for over 60 years.

McKusick Block, North Main Street. ca. May 1888, *Art Publishing Company,* Neenah, Wisconsin.
Ground-breaking on the McKusick block took place July 19, 1880. Tobacconist W. S. Conrad is at 102 North Main. A crockery and grocery store is on the right. The Odd Fellows hall was located on the ill-fated third story. A fire damaged the top floor and it stands today as two-story building. The Sawyer House can be seen at left.

Municipal Stillwater 3

"Sec. 1. Be it ordained by the City Council of the City of Stillwater, That if any hog shall be found running at large within the city limits of the City of Stillwater, it shall be the duty of the Marshal forthwith to take and impound such hog...
Passed April 27, 1854."
—John McKusick, Mayor

ON March 4, 1854, by an act of legislation, Stillwater was incorporated as a city in the Minnesota Territory. This meant that the newly formed city must have a local government and a city charter. These things did come about, and the citizens decided to have a Mayor-Council type of government. The first mayor elected was John McKusick, and the rest of the first council: J. C. York, J. N. Masterman, and C. Carli. They held their positions for one year, then another election took place. These people were chosen at large throughout the community. In 1873, the charter was changed and the council members were chosen from wards. The ward system continued until 1915, when once again the

council was chosen at large. In 1992, the city went back to the ward system. In 1881, the charter was amended to increase the term of the Mayor from one year, to two. In 1915 the term was again increased, from two to four years.

The following is a list of all those who have served as Mayor of the City of Stillwater and when they served:

STILLWATER MAYORS

Year	Mayor
1854	John McKusick (1815-1900)
1855	John Fisher (1825-1904)
1856	William Willim (1821-1895)
1857	Albert Stimson (1817-1898)
1858	A. B. Gorgas
1859	Rev. T. M. Fullerton (1817-1889)
1860-61	Mahlon Black (1820-1901)
1862	Francis R. Delano (1823-1887)
1863-64	David Bronson (1834-1919)
1865	William Grover
1866-67	William Willim (1821-1895)
1868	Charles J. Butler (1822-1894)
1869-70	William Holcombe (1804-1870)
1871-72	William McKusick (1825-1904)
1873	Alpheus K. Doe (1837-1907)
1874-75	W. G. Bronson (1843-1912)
1876	William McClure (1831-1890)
1877	Edward W. Durant (1829-1918)
1877-80	John S. Proctor (1826-1897)
1881-84	Samuel Matthews (1832-1906)
1885-86	Hollis R. Murdock (1832-1891)
1887-88	George M. Seymour (1829-1892)
1889-91	Edward W. Durant (1829-1918)

Page 38: Chestnut and Main Streets. ca. 1904.

Stillwater's street car system provided a quick and easy means of getting around town. When a branch was extended from Willernie in 1899, the railroads felt the pinch. However, by the late 1920s, both rail systems took a beating from buses and automobiles which were more mobile and met the needs of individual travelers better. Stillwater's street car line ended in August 1932 with a black creped funeral procession.

Adam Marty (1837-1923)
ca. 1875.

A Civil War veteran, when Marty was not acting as a civic leader, fireman or GAR activist, he was a sign and carriage painter.

1892-96	Charles A. Staples (1843-1911)
1896-99	A. W. Pattee (1835-?)
1900-09	James G. Armson (1859-1940)
1910-11	James W. Foley (1861-1933)
1912-13	Byron J. Mosier (1847-1933)
1914-15	Nick Starkel (1873-1938)
1915-20	Jacob Kolliner (1864-1933)
1920-22	William Smithson (1870-1922)
1922	M. Lee Murphy (1856-1934)
1922-26	R. J. Coffeen (1864-1971)
1926-30	George A. Sheils (1889-1961)
1930-34	Peter C. Lund (1881-1948)
1934-38	Fred B. Merrill (1886-1948)
1938-46	Runo G. Brodeen (1890-1952)
1946-50	Ed C. Carlson (1895-1974)
1950-54	E. W. Linner (1892-1969)
1954-62	Andrew Madsen (1893-1964)
1962-66	Dean Charlsen (1911-1986)
1966-74	William Powell (1919-)
1974-82	David 'Choc' Junker (1934-)
1982-86	Harry Peterson (1916-)
1986- 1993-	Wallace L. Abrahamson (1929-)

FIRE DEPARTMENT

The first attempt in organizing a city fire department came in 1859. On the evening of February 12, citizens met at Pugsley's Hall to discuss the formation of a fire company. W. H. Burt was chosen chairman of the

Stillwater Fire Department, on scene, 245 North Main Street. ca.1909, *John Runk Jr.*
Runk caught this blaze at P. N. Peterson's granite works as the building began to collapse. The fire started next door at a farm implement dealer and spread.

Roland F. Barnes (1863-1942)
ca. 1905.

Barnes was police chief in the early part of this century. After his stint in Stillwater, Barnes worked in Calumet, Michigan. He spent his retirement years back in Stillwater.

Fayette Castle (1881-1959)
ca. 1932.

Longtime police chief Castle is shown here with Stillwater's only police car.

meeting and a committee of three was chosen to draft a constitution and by-laws for the company. This company was ready to go if the city would provide an engine and the equipment for them to operate. However, the city, lacking enough funds to purchase the items needed, declined the offer of the company, and the company folded before starting. It wouldn't be until the early 1870s that Stillwater would get a permanent fire department.

The Silsby was purchased by the city for $7,350, and the fire department was organized with C. C. Johnson as Chief Engineer. Over 60 people signed up to volunteer their services in case of a fire.

The Fire House was built in 1887 and torn down to make way for the post office in 1966. The fire department is now a part of the Municipal Building located on North Fourth Street, across from the Public Library.

The following people have held the office of Fire Chief in the City of Stillwater:

STILLWATER FIRE CHIEFS

1872-83	David Bronson (1834-1919)
1883-95	Frank E. Joy (1842-1913)
1895-1907	Charles A. Johnson (1878-1918)
1907-10	Fred H. Thompson (-1917)
1910-12	Adolf R. Kelm

1912-40	James McGann (1858-1947)	1855	John Parker (1816-1867)
1940-55	John R. Colombo	1856	John Cilly
1955	Hoyt Elmquist	1857	Dennis Sullivan
1955-65	John Lawson (1920-)	1858	Robert Hastey
1965-70	Wilfred Cormier	1859	Thomas Sinclair (1833-1875)
1970-74	Paul G. Williams	1860-63	Duncan Chisholm
1974-88	David E. Chial	1864-65	John Shortall (1829-1888)
1988-	Gordy Siem (1944-)	1866	John May (1840-1895)
		1867	P. E. Keefe

POLICE DEPARTMENT

The police station was built in Stillwater during the summer of 1879 and located on the corner of Myrtle and Third Streets, at a cost of $6,150. The main building was twenty-eight by forty-five feet, and was two stories in height. The second floor was the municipal courtroom. In the rear of the building were twelve cells, each five by seven feet. This was Stillwater's police station until 1966, when the police moved to their new quarters in the Municipal Building on North Fourth Street. The old station was torn down to make way for the new post office, which opened in 1966.

The following people have held the position of Police Chief in the City of Stillwater:

STILLWATER POLICE CHIEFS

1854	Johnathan McKusick (1812-1876)	1868	John May (1840-1895)
		1869	John Shortall (1829-1888)
		1870	Harlow McIntyre (-1908)
		1871	Duncan Chisholm
		1872-73	John Lyons (1830-1909)
		1873-93	Mathew Shortall (1846-1903)
		1893-96	Granville Smith (1859-1907)
		1896-99	Frank M. Reeve
		1899-1905	John McIlree (1856-1905)
		1905-13	Roland F. Barnes (1863-1942)
		1913-29	W. E. McNaughton (1854-1929)
		1929-48	Fayette B. Castle (1881-1959)
		1948-49	Oscar L. Anderson
		1949-60	Raymond F. Law (1914-)
		1960-65	Eldon D. Sanders
		1965-67	Alf G. Roepke, Jr. (1923-)
		1967-84	Wallace L. Abrahamson (1919-)
		1984-92	David Mahowter (1949-)
		1992-	Don Beberg (1939-)

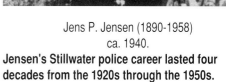

Jens P. Jensen (1890-1958)
ca. 1940.
Jensen's Stillwater police career lasted four decades from the 1920s through the 1950s.

OPPOSITE: Washington County Courthouse, clerk of court's office, 3rd & Pine Streets. February 13, 1904 *John Runk Jr.*

(L-R) Alpheus K. Doe (1837-1907), Charles T. Lammers, Alpheus E. Doe (1863-1930).

Washington County Historic Courthouse, 3rd and Pine Streets. 1992 *Dean R. Thilgen*

In 1975, after a new government center was completed, the fate of this Italiante landmark on Zion's hill was uncertain. Designed by St. Paul architect Augustus F. Knight, its original appearance had been covered by years of paint and remodeling, creating more of an eyesore than a functional building. The usefulness of the old courthouse was in doubt. However, after a campaign to save and restore the building, it continues today to be operated by the county as a meeting facility and historic display area. School children walk its halls to discover a part of Stillwater's past. Weddings and receptions in the former courtroom are booked many months in advance. Office space is leased to the American Red Cross, Valley Tours and other businesses. These adaptive uses affirm the viability of older, majestic buildings. It is on the National Register of Historic Places.

Lowell Park, along waterfront. 1947, *A. Pearson Company.*

In 1908 the city and the Booster Club announced plans to develop "Levee Park." Agreements with the Northern Pacific railway paved the way to its development, but it was Elmore Lowell who pushed the park plans ahead in 1909 with a $5,000 gift. Architect W. A. Finkelberg of Winona, Minnesota was hired to design the park which was renamed in Lowell's honor. Work began in June 1911. Park expansion plans were brought forth by Mr. Lowell in September 1914 under the design team of Morrell & Nichols. A revised plan was later implemented. The pavilion was completed in June 1923, another gift of Mr. Lowell. Other additions and changes were done in the 1930s and 1940s. Plans to revitalize and expand the park, which include a statue of Elmore Lowell, are underway at present.

McKUSICK LAKE PARK is a ⅓-acre park on Owens Street. It was created in 1989 from the remains of the teenagers' dike from the record flood of 1965. It includes a parking lot, a playground, and canoe access to McKusick Lake.

POST OFFICE PARK, situated across from the Lowell Inn on Second Street, was donated by the Farmer family in 1934 and was built the following year.

PIONEER PARK is located on the site of the Isaac Staples mansion on North Second Street. After the home was torn down the land was purchased by the city in 1935.

LOWELL PARK is located on the waterfront. Elmore Lowell was instrumental in the funding and creation of the park. It is slated for a well-needed renovation and expansion.

KOLLINER PARK (also known as Legion Beach), a 49-acre park located across the river was originally developed in the 1920s. In 1931, the swimming beach was added as a project of the city and the American Legion.

LILY LAKE RECREATIONAL CENTER is an 11-acre park on Greeley Street which was purchased in three segments in 1922, 1951 and in the late 1960s.

Lily Lake Beach, South Greeley Street. 1962, *A. Pearson Company*.
The Veterans Memorial beach and beachhouse on the south shore of Lily Lake was created in 1948 under the leadership of George Kunz. Today, tennis courts, softball fields, a boat launch, and an indoor ice rink are part of the recreational complex completed in 1971.

TRIANGLE PARK is a small triangular plot given to the city in 1888 to forgive a $66 assessment against the owner, Daniel Hurley. The city took and forgave Mr. Hurley, and the small land on South Broadway became one of the first city parks.

WASHINGTON PARK is probably the oldest park in the city. An 1874 map lists "Washington Square" at the corner of Western Row (Greeley Street) and Pennock Street (Churchill Street).

Opening of bridge, July 1, 1931.
(L-R) Brig. Gen. Ralph Immel, Cal Karnestad of KSTP radio, not identified, Gov. Floyd B. Olson, William Madden, and not identified.
The new bridge not only meant a safer passage of boats, but also a toll-free highway link between Minnesota and Wisconsin, something taken for granted today.

Plaque unveiling ceremony, Stillwater convention Centennial celebration. August 25, 1948, *Carl Ermisch.*

McKusick's store was the site of the 1848 Territorial Convention. This building was located at the corner of Myrtle and Main Streets. In 1911 the Wolf Building was built on the same location, and it is here that this group gathered to witness the unveiling of a plaque noting the convention site. Photographer Carl Ermisch caught Jean R. Emmanuelson singing the national anthem. Director William H. Bastien and the Municipal Band are seated on a platform to the right.

Stillwater Prison, North Main Street. ca. 1898, *Dorge,* Minneapolis, Minnesota.

Stillwater Penatenturies 4

"Who enters here, leaves all hope behind."
—old prison slogan

ON January 16, 1851, a bill was introduced which located the Capitol of Minnesota Territory at St. Paul and the territorial prison at Stillwater. At no recorded time did Stillwater's legislators ever have a "choice" in picking one state institution over another.

Congress appropriated $20,000 for the construction of the prison. It was built in the part of Stillwater known as "Battle Hollow," named that because of the battle that took place there between the Dakota and the Ojibwa in July 1839. The buildings of the prison and the warden's residence were completed in 1853.

The first warden to look over the prison was Frank R. Delano who served until 1858. Delano's administration was extremely corrupt. Escapes were numerous and prisoners were let out of prison when counties failed to pay the amount of money to keep the prisoners incarcerated. Because of these, and other duty failures, Frank Smith took over as warden. Smith, however, resigned several months later and was replaced by Henry N. Setzer who served until 1860.

John S. Proctor was appointed to the post in 1860 and made some changes in identifying prisoners. Before Proctor became warden, inmates were identified by having half their heads shaved. As the prison population grew, Proctor instituted "penitentiary stripes" for the prisoners to wear as clothing for easier identification. Proctor also applied for larger facilities because the prison had reached its maximum capacity by 1862.

The necessary appropriation having been made, steps were taken to enlarge the grounds and erect more commodious buildings. The contract for building a dry house and shops, costing $14,500 dollars, was awarded to a Stillwater firm by the name of Seymour, Sabin & Co. on May 3, 1869. During that construction, the walls were extended, enclosing nine and one-half acres.

Replacing Warden Proctor was Joshua L. Taylor, from Taylors Falls, in 1868; he was followed by A. C. Webber for less than one year in 1870. Henry A. Jackman followed

North Main Street showing deputy warden's house, warden's house, prison wall with guard tower and cell block. ca. 1900.
The warden's house has been placed on the National Register of Historic Places. Today it is a museum of the Washington County Historical Society. The base of the guard tower is also still intact. The main cellblock and administration office behind was removed around 1936. The deputy warden's house at left is also gone.

Warden Webber, and it was under Jackman that the principal building was erected at a cost of $74,000. This building was enlarged several years later for another $5,000.

In the late 1850s, the labor of the convicts were leased to private industries. John B. Stevens, a Stillwater manufacturer of shingles, leased the prison workshop and took over convict labor. Two years later, Stevens' mill burned down, and he went

bankrupt. The convict labor then went to George Seymour, later mayor of Stillwater, and William Webster. Their company produced flour barrels and in the late 1860s, they were joined by Dwight M. Sabin, who later became a U.S. Senator from Minnesota. The firm then became known as Seymour, Sabin and Company. They controlled the convict labor for twenty years, when finally enough people were outraged by the unfair-

ness of this cheap labor that the Minnesota State Legislature pass legislation prohibiting the use of prison labor in direct competition with free enterprise. This caused the state in 1891 to start their own industries to keep the prisoners busy. The first of these new businesses was the making of twine, and it continued in the present facility until 1971.

John A. Reed became warden on August 3, 1874, and stayed thirteen years when

H. J. Stordock was appointed in Reed's place. It was during Reed's administration, however, that the prison received it's most infamous prisoners: the Younger Brothers in 1876. The Younger brothers (Cole, Jim and Bob) were captured near Madelia, Minnesota after they and the James brothers attempted to rob the Northfield, Minnesota bank. They were sentenced to life imprisonment after pleading guilty to murder in the first degree. However, the Youngers became model prisoners, and it was these Younger's that helped establish the *Prison Mirror,* an inmate newspaper started with inmate funds and published by the prisoners. It is now the oldest continuously published prison paper in the nation.

Albert Garvin took over as warden on January 2, 1891, and served only until the following June. Henry Wolfer was appointed and served in that position until 1915, except for the period of December 1899, through March 1901, when General Charles McC. Reeve filled the warden's chair.

With the prison population increasing beyond its capacity, (total number of prisoners topped 700 in 1905) the state legislature set aside funds in 1905 and 1909 to build a new facility just south of Stillwater. The new state prison was opened for business in November 1908. The last prisoners were transferred to the new prison in 1914. Warden Wolfer continued as the warden in the new prison for one year, then retired.

The old prison buildings were used as storage and warehouses until the mid-1930s when they were systematically torn down, with the stone being used to line the Mississippi River from St. Paul to Red Wing to help ease the erosion of the river bank.

The old warden's residence served as a state house until 1941, when then Governor of Minnesota, Harold Stassen, signed the house over to the Washington County Historical Society. It continues to be used as the county museum to collect, store, and display the history of Washington County, Minnesota.

With the prison population still growing, the state of Minnesota built and opened a Maximum Security Prison in Oak Park Heights, Minnesota in 1982, in which only the most dangerous prisoners from across the state are put. The prison in Bayport, Minnesota is now only for minimum security prisoners.

WARDENS OF STILLWATER TERRITORIAL PRISON

1853-58	Francis R. Delano (1823-1887)
1858	Francis O. J. Smith (1825-1891)
1858-60	Henry N. Setzer (1825-1898)
1860-68	John S. Proctor (1826-1897)
1868-70	Joshua L. Taylor
1870	A. C. Webber
1870-74	Henry A. Jackman (1819-1889)
1874-87	John A. Reed (1831-1910)
1887-91	H. G. Stordock
1891-92	Albert Garvin (1851-1924)
1892-99	Henry Wolfer (1853-1919)
1899-1901	Charles McC. Reeve
1901-14	Henry Wolfer (1853-1919)

OVERLEAF: Stillwater prison , warden's house and Minnesota Thresher company on North Main Street. Taken from Laurel Street steps. ca. April 1888, *Art Publishing Compay,* Neenah, Wisconsin.

(Page 55): Warden Henry Wolfer (1853-1919) in office. 1899

Interstate bridge under water, 1965 flood. April 17, 1965, *St. Paul Pioneer Press (Ted).*

Disasters 5

"The gutters became babbling brooks, then increased to rapid streams and a few seconds later had swolen to rivers that carried everything before them irresistible at the speed of a mill race..."
—Stillwater *Gazette, May 10, 1894*

FIRE OF 1866

In the early morning of December 26, 1866, twelve buildings on Stillwater's Main Street, burned to the ground. The fire originated between the Weinschenk and Curtis Buildings by a falling ember from a nearby chimney. After the fire, only five buildings remained standing in that part of town.

Firefighting had not been organized yet, so a water bucket brigade was used. A steam fire engine would not become a part of the Stillwater's firefighting equipment for another five and one-half years.

PRISON FIRES OF 1884

On January 7, 1884, fire broke out in the Northwestern Car Company shops in the prison. The buildings that caught fire, which were only fifty feet away from prison cell blocks, included pattern shops, hardwood & softwood shops, and the engine room. Gus Lindahl, a watchman whose duty it was to watch the steam heating and water supply, discovered the fire in the glazing room on the third floor of the wood shops at around 10:45 P.M. Lindahl, with the help of another watchman, John Walton, attempted to put out the fire without success and quickly sounded the alarm. The fire department was called out, but by the time they arrived, flames were coming out the windows in the four story building. After the flames were put out, about 300 men lost their jobs and damage was estimated a $300,000.

Later that month, on January 25, the prison caught on fire again. Soon the massive structure was engulfed in flames. The prisoners were still inside the cell blocks, and the deputy warden was told to take 25 of the most trusted prisoners and give then arms to help escort the other prisoners out of the fire. Among these 25 prisoners included the notorious Youngers. All but one of the prisoners were taken to safety; Henry Lemple suffocated and died in his cell. Total damage was estimated at $20,000.

By eight o'clock the next morning, Company K and soldiers from St. Paul had arrived to take care of the situation. The prisoners were taken to various parts of the state until the prison was repaired. The

Aftermath of prison fire. January 1884, *John M. Kuhn.*

The two photos appear to be of the second fire that overtook the cell block on January 26. The left shot shows the massive and total destruction of one building. The right shot is thought to be from Main Street, showing the destruction to the main building. One prisoner was not released and died in his cell. Well-known photographer John M. Kuhn took several stereoscopic views of the disaster. Both are from the right-half of the stereo card.

Younger brothers were taken to the Washington County Courthouse for four weeks, the only time during their time in prison that they were outside the prison walls.

FLOODS OF 1885

On June 12, 1885, heavy rains flooded Stillwater, but it was nothing compared to what would occur just two days later. Sunday night, June 14th, the skies opened up and dropped even more rain on the already soaked city.

The Sawyer House, the largest hotel in Stillwater at the time, had water pour into the dining room. The entire first floor had between two to three feet of water in it, and, at one scary moment, a boulder weighing about one hundred pounds crashed through the hotel's barber shop and came to rest against a stove in the next room. The Pitman House, another hotel located on North Third Street, also had their dinning room swamped with three feet of water. Damage to the Pitman House was about $3500.

Dr. Pratt and Dr. Clark lost their medical libraries and their surgical instruments were ruined as well, all valued at $2000. Thomas Sutton lost his home and his small candy store, which was located on Myrtle Street. R.B. Chapman's meat market on Main

Street became the final resting place for a lot of the displaced dirt and sand. The pile in front of the market was about six feet deep.

In all, about $25,000 in damage was caused by the cloud burst.

FLOODS OF 1894

A great flood occurred on May 9, 1894. Most of the damage took place on Myrtle Street, which some say took the form of a tidal wave. The water swept a small building down stream and carried three people with it. Two the people were washed aside, but the other, Charles H. Lilligren, was pinned under some timber and broke his leg. He was saved before sliding into the St. Croix River, but his injuries where so severe that he died the next morning.

The paving on Myrtle Street was ripped up, with the rushing water sending the paving blocks tumbling down the street toward the St. Croix, coming to rest on the railroad tracks. The Sawyer House, located at Myrtle and Second Street, suffered $2000 worth of damage. Water stood five to six feet deep in the dinning room, barber shop, and billiard room of the hotel, depositing sand and mud everywhere.

The Stillwater Gas and Light Company suffered the heaviest losses. The water,

mud, and sand, destroyed the machinery, causing $25,000 of damage. Other businesses that suffered heavy losses were: Brewer Frank Aiple, $5000; Minnesota Thresher Company, $2000; and Stillwater Water Company, $1000. The total estimate of the damage was over $100,000.

BRIDGE FIRE OF 1904

On Thursday September 15, 1904, at about three o'clock in the afternoon the east span of the wooden pontoon bridge that spanned the St. Croix from Stillwater to Wisconsin burned.

The fire department reached the bridge and was followed by a large crowd of spectators. The firemen and crowd went onto the burning span, and with all that weight and the fire raging, the span collapsed, sending all into the river. Many were pinned under the fallen timbers of the bridge. Assistance came as soon as possible, but not soon enough for 22 year old Adolph Boo, who was killed by falling debris. Others had to be cut out of the maze of lumber including George McGrath, age 16, who was severely injured and died the following morning. Some of the others that were injured included Assistant Fire Chief

ABOVE AND RIGHT: Flash flood damage at North 4th & Hickory Streets. May 10, 1894.
Hickory Street ends at North 4th Street. In the flash flood of May 9, 1894 a house and barn at the foot of Hickory was washed down the ravine.

James McGann, Ed McPheters, Ray French, Joe Decurtins, and Herman Wojohn.

The east span of the bridge was a total loss. It took several weeks to repair the bridge, and during that time a ferry boat from Hudson, Wisconsin took people across the St. Croix.

BRINE'S FIRE OF JANUARY 1982

On Friday January 22, 1982, a cold winter night, a fire broke out at Brine's Meat Market in downtown Stillwater. This fire would be the largest loss of life in more than 75 years.

The fire quickly engulfed the meat market and spread next door to the Country Tailor clothing store. Three firemen went to the roof of the clothing store to try to vent the fire. At about quarter to midnight, the roof collapsed, sending the three men into the blaze.

Two of the firemen, Bruce S. Raeburn and Robert B. Hayes, both of Mahtomedi, Minnesota, did not escape the flames and perished in the fire. The other, Kevin Charlsen, of Stillwater, landed on a ledge in the store and did not get directly into the fire. Stillwater Fire Chief Gordy Seim said, "It was an inferno (inside The Country Tailor). How Charlsen ever survived I don't know." Two

other Stillwater fire fighters also received injuries; volunteer Tim Bell, with smoke inhalation, and regular Bob Barthol, who was hit by debris in the Country Tailor. Both men were treated at Lakeview Memorial Hospital in Stillwater.

There were four fire departments were called in to fight this blaze. Brine's Meat Market rebuilt and to the joy of the Brine family, the 16 star American Flag which was displayed proudly in the restaurant, was not damaged and now is once again displayed in the building.

FLOOD OF 1952

On April 15, 1952, the St. Croix River was at the highest level in recorded history. The river was measured at 689.48 feet above sea level, which surpassed the previous record of 689.47, recorded in 1850. Water completely covered Chestnut Street between the railroad tracks and the interstate bridge. Sandbags were placed around the Maple Island, Inc. main building and some Omaha Railroad property near the river.

STILLWATER HIGH SCHOOL FIRE OF 1957

On Monday night, December 23, 1957, the old high school building was completely

destroyed by fire. At around 6 P.M., several people discovered the fire and called the fire department. Firemen were at the scene at once, and found the school engulfed in flames. There were several explosions in the building, which hampered the fire fighting efforts. It took more than 90 firemen and volunteers to put the fire out.

The total loss in the fire was estimated at $250,000. The department with the heaviest losses was the music department. George Regis, the high school band director, estimated a $10,000 loss in music alone. Also lost were 2 saxophones, 4 sousaphones, several other instruments and about a dozen band uniforms. Three thousand books in the school library were also burned.

The students resumed classes on January 6, 1958. Classroom space was offered by several churches, the city armory, and by Warden Rigg of the state prison. A new high school was built in 1960.

GRAND OPERA HOUSE FIRE OF 1902

On the morning of December 5, 1902, the Grand Opera House was totally destroyed, and the adjoining Holcombe and Disch Blocks badly damaged by fire.

At a little after three o'clock in the morning, fire was discovered in the second

Aftermath of High School fire, Pine and 3rd Streets. December 24, 1957, *Roger Peterson.*
The sudden destruction of the old High School was an emotional one for all SHS students and graduates. The 1887 part of the school was completely gutted. It also left the school district without a functional high school. The citizens pulled together and found rooms around town to hold classes until a new school could be built.

floor of the Opera House near the stage. The fire department was called, but by the time they reached the Opera House, the building was engulfed in flames. The walls of the Opera House crumbled and fell into the street. The fire spread to the buildings next door, the Holcome and Disch blocks.

A message was sent to St. Paul for help with the fire. A company was dispatched, and arrived by special train at 6 A.M. with an engine and hose cart with fifteen men. By that time, the fire was under control and the engine and cart were never unloaded from the train.

The total damage of the fire amounted to over $150,000. No lives were lost, but for a short time there was concern that Nicholas Clark, who lived beneath the stage, had not made it out of the building. He was found behind the building, getting out just before the walls caved in.

Some of the businesses with the heaviest losses in the fire were: Ziegler Bros. clothing store—$40,000; J.O. Holen & Co., a grocery store—$20,000; and Emil Okerblad's photography studio—$3,000.

FLOOD OF 1965

In the early spring of 1965, the valley experienced unusually heavy rainfall. This added to heavy snow runoff and raised the St. Croix River well above flood stage. Knowing the devastation that surely would occur without their help, St. Croix Valley residents, school children, and 50 inmates from the correctional facility farm colony teamed together. Starting April 10, they built a dike to save the downtown area. From a large painted sign placed by the hundreds of young people shoveling sand, this dike became known as the "Teenager's Dike."

The river finally crested at 694.07 feet above sea level. The flood was not only unique because of the water level, but because people joined together to save the community. Roger Peterson, a city councilman during the flood, recalled that he received a call from a Minneapolis man at 6 A.M. Easter morning and wanted to know if it would be all right if he came over with a car load of other volunteers and help in any way he could. Peterson responded by saying "Sure come on over!" The man on the phone was blind.

City hall. 8:05 A.M., April 18, 1965.
At the height of the floodwaters, the flood command center was manned by city council members, Red Cross volunteers and St. Croix Valley C.B. Club volunteers. (L-R) Red Cross volunteer Tom Dewhurst, Roger Peterson, Don Nolde, E. O. (Tiny) Iverson, and members of the St. Croix Valley C.B. Club.

Teenager's dike, 1965 flood workers. April 15, 1965, *St. Paul Pioneer Press (Young).*
As this photo shows, no one was too young to help save the town. School children, prisoners and concerned citizens from miles around all lent a hand.

Chestnut Street at Main Street, 1965 flood. April 17, 1965, *St. Paul Pioneer Press (Ted).*
Downtown Stillwater was closed off to the general public for a few days. Due to careful planning, the downtown business district was spared any serious damage.

Amusements 6

"Stillwater, Minnesota, a plucky little town, just admitted to the Northwestern League, raised $10,300 towards supporting the new club, in just three hours and-a-half."
—The Sporting Life, *January 23, 1884*

STILLWATER was a rapidly growing town during the 1840s. With the territorial convention completed and Minnesota becoming a territory, Stillwater had thrust itself into a leading city of this newly formed area. With the population becoming larger, more free time was being found and things to fill that time became necessary. In 1850, Stillwater had a visit from the Antonio Brothers, one of many circuses and carnivals to come over the next seventy years. During a visit of the Cooper & Bailey's Circus in 1876, a team of wild horses ran down Third Street, and when turning onto Chestnut Street, the wagon turned over, killing the driver. Stillwater even became a brief childhood home to the five Ringling Brothers, who would go on and develop the Greatest Show on Earth.

After the Civil War, the "national pastime" found its way into the St. Croix Valley. In 1868, a local baseball club was formed and called itself the St. Croix Club. This club became one of the most powerful teams in the state. They won the state championship that fall by winning two of three games from the Northfield Club. The St. Croix Club continued for more than a decade, entertaining the crowds in Stillwater and throughout the state. It was, however, in 1876, that the club had its greatest thrill. During that year, the team took on the National Champion Chicago White Stockings, who were led by Adrian Anson.

The St. Croix Club did well, but the professional club proved too much, defeating the local boys by the score of 18-3.

In 1883, a new semi-professional team was formed in Stillwater called the Minnesota Chiefs. The Chiefs had a very successful year, and this lead local investors to form a truly professional team the following year. They were admitted to the Northwestern League which consisted of teams from six states.

Stillwater's 1884 club signed its first player, John W. "Bud" Fowler, a black man, to play that year. Fowler would prove to be the most able player and the only negro in the Northwestern League that year. The team itself lost its first sixteen games and

Page 68: VFW Halloween Party, Stillwater Armory. October 31, 1945, *Carl Ermisch.*
650 kids and parents packed the Stillwater Armory for a Halloween party sponsored by the Veterans of Foreign Wars. George Muller was master of ceremonies and James Tibbetts assisted by entertaining everyone with clown antics. Carl Johnson also appeared as a Keystone Cop. A talent show was held and George Flynn's piano playing took first prize.

The costume winners were (L-R): Darlene Schell as an old lady, Pamela Palmer as a tramp, Peter Schinn as a clown, Joe Charlsen as a cowboy, and Leona Ruline as a woman from the old days. Each won a best or funniest category for costume.

OPPOSITE: Log rolling contest on the St. Croix River. ca. 1903, *Frank T. Wilson.*

folded before the year was over. However, eleven players from the Stillwater club would go on to play in the major leagues.

As the 1890s came, Stillwater businesses began sponsoring local clubs, such as the Joseph Wolf Brewery, the Bazar stores, and Simonet Furniture Company. These teams played other business sponsored clubs throughout the state and even some Wisconsin clubs.

Baseball took another turn in Stillwater with the founding of the Stillwater Loggers in 1933. The club played until 1965 and during that time produced some great minor league ball players. Some of these players include Neil Junker, Frank Stewart, Mark Crimmins, Arne Flaa, and Bud Grant. The only native born Stillwater resident to make the major leagues was a man named James Hollis Rutherford, who played one game in the outfield for the Cleveland Indians in 1910.

The Stillwater High School turned out two championship teams: in 1902 they won the N.I.A.A. (National Interscholastic Athletic Association), and 89 years later, in 1991, they won the Class AA state championship.

In 1884, a new sport took over the citizens of Stillwater—rollerskating. On April 23, 1884, the Stillwater Roller Rink opened to an enthusiastic crowd of between 800-900 people. About 150 skaters glided along the birch floor of the new rink, while Mr. Crocker, an expert skater of the world, performed for the crowd. Manager Parmelee of the roller rink, set aside the hours of ten until noon so that ladies could practice their skating "unobserved by the other sex." Later that year on May 28, W. D. Wilmot, a noted bicyclist of the time, stopped in Stillwater to perform one show at the new rink. The roller rink lasted for a couple years, then went out of business. The building was destroyed by fire on April 9, 1889.

Wintertime found new and different amusements for the citizens of the St. Croix Valley. In 1886, the toboggan club was organized in Stillwater. Alderman J. C. Kilty asked the City Council that a hill be designated for such a slide. The slide was on South Second Street and was about 100 feet long. With an angle of 45 degrees, the hill gave a slide of almost 500 feet. The slide attracted large crowds through the month of March. There were several accidents that occurred. One was when a toboggan tipped over, and the rider lost part of an ear. The slide soon melted, and in the March 25, 1886 Stillwater *Gazette,* it

Mark Crimmins
1947
Crimmins signed to play with the New York Yankees class D ball team in Fond Du Lac, Wisonsin. He played one year, then injury forced him to retire from the game professionally.

stated that "the toboggan slide is now a sweet memory of the past."

Stillwater's cultural set would not be denied their fun, so in August, 1879, work began on the construction of the Grand Opera House. It was designed by the famous Minneapolis architect Radcliff. The building fronted Main Street and was 120feet deep. The entire cost of the building was $75,000 taking less than two years to construct. The Salsbury's Troubadours performed for the formal opening on May 11, 1881. Seats for the show ranged from 50 cents to 100 dollars.

Many of the best plays and operas of the day would make Stillwater's Grand Opera House a stop on their tours. John Philip Sousa's band played there as well as boxing exhibitions by the World Champion bare-knuckle boxer John L. Sullivan in 1883 and 1886. On September 26, 1881, Buffalo Bill brought his Wild West Show to Stillwater and the Grand Opera House.

The building and its entire contents were destroyed by fire during the night of December 5, 1902. The building's remains were purchased by the Simonet Brothers who still have their furniture store in what was once the grandest of all opera houses in the area.

Golf came to Stillwater in 1924 from an idea created at a Stillwater Rotary Club meeting. On September 24, 1924, a public meeting was held to discuss plans for a Stillwater golf course. Four possible sites for the course were found, so the assistance of Tom Vardon was received to help pick the site. His credentials included serving as the golf professional at the White Bear Yacht club and brother of the famous English golfer Harry Vardon. An area on the North Hill, called "Atwood's Field" was chosen, and Vardon laid out the nine hole course. The club opened for play in April, 1925. The membership grew, and in 1943 the course started a Labor Day match-play event that has grown into one of the largest in the state. The tournament is now called the Lyle Cran Memorial Shortstop, named for the long serving greenskeeper of the Stillwater Country Club.

In the 1950s, the course was expanded to eighteen holes. The club hired architect Paul Coates to design the new nine, and by the end of that decade, all eighteen holes of the course were in excellent shape.

Stillwater's turf was also used in a different manner at one time. On Tuesday, July 22, 1873, the Lily Lake Driving Park Association was formed after it was an-

Bazar baseball team. 1900, *Emil Okerblad.*
Many businesses in the 1890s as well as into the 20th century sponsored city baseball clubs. Such businesses in Stillwater included the Joseph Wolf Company, Simonet's, and the Bazar clothing store. The 1900 Bazar club had a winning season playing teams such as the West Publishing Company from St. Paul, the St. Paul Colts, the St. Paul Cheavers, and clubs from Hudson and Rice Lake, Wisconsin. The team lost to Rice Lake 16-2. In explaining the loss, Bazar player Jerry Crimmins said the "Rice Lake pitcher put them over the plate like rifle balls and the Bazars thought the balls looked as small as a marble." He also claimed the fielders had some trouble, getting a case of the "rattles." The fielders were "kept chasing leather all over the field until the end of the game." The Bazar's pitcher Walter Yorks did strikeout fourteen batters.
(L-R) Standing: Tut Voligny, Clem Arndt, Dan Callahan, George Voligny, George Grady, Henry Defew, Jerry Crimmins. Seated: Fred LeClaire, Elmer Laun, Walter Yorks.

Stillwater High School baseball team. 1902, *Gustav Halmrast.*
The Stillwater High School have won many championships, but one of the first titles for Stillwater came in 1902 when the High School baseball team captured the pennant of the N.I.A.A. (National Interscholastic Athletic Association). The Stillwater Club won the first game it played on April 28, defeating the East Side High School of Minneapolis by the score of 20-6. The team would only lose one game, that to Cleveland High School of St. Paul, but that loss was protested because semi-professional players played with Cleveland High School's team. Stillwater's protest was granted, and the game was thrown out, and thus Stillwater High School's baseball team won the pennant of 1902 with an unbeaten record. The team leaders in batting that year were: Ned Easton (.385), Jay Crowley (.318), and Roy Borrowman (.308).
(L-R) Back row: Rob McDonald, Everett Burns, Rob McKellar, Joy Davis, John Conklin. Middle row: Ned Easton, Jay Crowley, Cliff Booren, Stephen Clark. Front: Roy Borrowman, Earle Castle.

Grand Opera House ceiling fresco. ca. 1882, *John M. Kuhn.*
Six frescoers and decorators from Chicago began working on the ceiling and walls in March 1881. The top-center figure represents the guardian spirit of fine arts, with the Muses of painting, poetry and architecture to the left and music and dramatic theatre on the right.

Grand Opera House, South Main Street. ca. April 1888, *Art Publishing Co., Neenah, Wisconsin.*
The Grand Opera House opened May 11, 1881. It was a stopping point for many traveling performers and speakers. By extending the stage, masquerades were also held regularly.

nounced that Mr. P. Schulenberg and Isaac Staples purchased 130 acres of land on the shores of Lily Lake for $6,000. By September, the race track was one of the best in the Midwest. The Third Annual Washington County Fair was held at the site, and over $800 in prize money was offered for the races.

Over the years of racing at the Lily Lake race track, many state and national champions raced there. Some of them were Gol Ricely, owned by J. S. O'Brien; Zig, owned by Isaac Staples; Edna Patch, Dan Patch's grand dame; and even Dan Patch himself.

On October 31, 1902, the buildings on the race track grounds were destroyed by fire. In 1903, the race track property was inherited by Mary Bell Toule, Isaac Staples granddaughter. She then sold the property to the Benson family, which still owns the property today.

Several performing theaters operated in the early part of this century. The Auditorium Theater on 2nd Street opened January 27, 1906. The Novelty Theater on South Main was re-opened as the Majestic Theater July 4, 1908. Both theaters added motion pictures around 1914. The Majestic began running ads for the "photo play" serial "The Broken Coin" in November 1915.

Skipper crew for Play Day 1953. July 30, 1953, *John Runk Jr.*
(L-R) Top row: Margery Schadegg, Ann Kilty, Georgine Howalt, Rosemary Bolline, Roberta Ecker, Frances Roloff, Mary McGlinch, Mary Jo Bjorkman, and Jerry Heany. Seated: Maxine Gardner, Arlene Larson, Jean White, Donna Chapin, Darlene Schell and Nancy Fehlow.
Darlene Schell was crowned skipper, Mary McGlinch was chosen as first mate and Ann Kilty as second mate.

Play Day was an outgrowth of the success of the 1948 Stillwater Convention Centennial celebration. Its first year was 1949 and over the years grew from one day in length to several days. The last Play Days was in 1965. In 1968, Mr. & Mrs. Robert Thompson led the way to the revival of the Lumberjack Days celebration that was originally held in the 1930s and early 1940s. The annual event recalls the lumbering heritage of Stillwater's old days. Lumberjack Days is taking a hiatus in 1993.

Steamer Kalitan and touring barge Markitana, levee next to Lowell Park. ca. 1931, *A. Pearson Compay.*
These privately-owned boats plied the waters of the St. Croix frequently during the 1930s.

Stillwater Country Club. ca. 1925, *John Runk Jr.*
This view looks across the ninth green to the clubhouse. Note the sprinkler system in use. The course is considered to be one of the most challenging in Minnesota.

Ice cream social, Schulenberg Community Club at old Schulenberg school. August 1, 1948, *St. Paul Pioneer Press (Hi Paul)*.

The Schulenberg Community Club used the retired Schulenberg schoolhouse as a neighborhood center. (L-R) Arthur G. Nelson, president of the club, and Herbert Callies, recreation club president, hang Japanese lanterns of the real and homemade kind as part of an ice cream social to raise money for area parks.

Children at Central School playground. 1912, *John Runk Jr.*

This photo was part of a series used in a Stillwater School District booklet. A "staged" version of this scene made it into the book as well as photos of the city's school buildings and classrooms. The school yard equipment appears to be keeping everyone rather involved in play.

Classroom at St. Michael's School, South 3rd Street. ca. 1920.

Churches and Schools 7

"Too little attention has been given to the development of good penmanship in the public schools."
Manual and Courses of Study of Stillwater Public Schools, 1911-1912.

IN 1842, the first religious sermon was given at the Tamarack House, in the trading post of Dakotah. This sermon was given by a traveling preacher, the Rev. Hurlbert. A few weeks later, the Rev. Brace delivered another sermon at the same home.

In 1844, the Rev. William T. Boutwell held services at McKusick's boarding house, and Boutwell became a resident of Stillwater a few years later. Boutwell helped organize the **First Presbyterian Church** on December 8, 1849.

The First Presbyterian Church building was dedicated in August 1851. On the evening of June 25, 1866, a terrible thunderstorm swept across Stillwater. The storm's fierce winds toppled the church building,

sending the steeple crashing into Myrtle Street. A new church was built on the corner of Third and Myrtle Streets. The present First Presbyterian Church of Stillwater sanctuary on Osgood Avenue was built in 1968.

The first pastor of the Presbyterian Church was the Rev. Henry M. Nichols who served until the Spring of 1860. Other pastors of the church were; the Rev. J. S. Howell (1860-1863), the Rev. E. B. Wright (1863-1873), the Rev. I. N. Otis (1874-1877), the Rev. A. A. Kiehle (1877-1881), the Rev. J. H. Carroll (1881-1887), the Rev. W. H. Albright (1887), the Rev. L. H. Morey (1887-1892), the Rev. J. LeMoyne Danner (1892-97), the Rev. S. J. Kennedy (1892-1908), the Rev. John McCoy (1908-1916), the Rev. Gilbert L. Wil-

son (1917-1920), the Rev. Arthur W. Ratz (1920-1925), the Rev. Clement D. Loehr (1925-1929), the Rev. Jackson E. Smith (1929-1938), the Rev. Carl O. Olson (1938-1943), the Rev. A. Garland Rotenberry (1944-1945), the Rev. Paul Fletcher Smith (1955-1965), the Rev. Merle E. Strohbehn (1965-1977), the Rev. William R. Chadwick (1977-1984). The more recent pastors are: Richard Ryman, Anita Cummings, Rebecca Tollefson, Richard Knowles, Herbert A. Miller (interim Pastor, 1991), and presently the Rev. David A. Hansen.

The **Second Presbyterian Church** was organized on November 26, 1856 by William Holcombe and others with Holcombe acting as elder and one of the trustees, and the Rev. J. C. Caldwell as pastor.

The church got off to a rough start. When the church building was about completed, in 1857, it burned to the ground. A small building was erected on land purchased on Churchill and Nelson Streets. the Rev. Caldwell resigned his post in 1869 After several other pastors had come and gone, the Second Presbyterian Church merged with the First Presbyterian Church in 1877.

St. Michael's Catholic Church was organized in 1852. In 1853, Father Daniel J. Fisher erected a small frame church on North Fourth Street. Father Fisher, who left in 1856 and later became president of Seton Hall College, was succeeded by Father Thomas Murray, who enlarged the small church building.

In 1870, after the death of Father Murray, Father Maurice E. Murphy took over as pastor and helped in the construction of a new building at the corner of South Third and Walnut Streets. Construction began in 1873 and completed in 1875.

Father Murphy continued as pastor until resigning in 1891. Father Charles E. Corcoran took over and remained until his death in 1943. Other pastors that followed include: Father Daniel J. MacCarthy (1943-1955), Father Francis J. Miller (1955-1968), Father Richard V. Berg (1969-1977), Father Thomas Fitzgerald (1977-1987), Father Leo Huber (1987), Father Robert Patterson (1987-89), Father John Szarke (1990-91), Father Michael Skluzacek (1992-present).

St. Mary's Catholic Church was organized in March 1865 as **Immaculate Conception Catholic Church**. The old Presbyterian Church on Third Street was purchased and used for services until a larger building was needed. The first pastor of the church was the Rev. Aloysius Plut.

In 1871, the congregation purchased five lots on Fifth and Pine Streets and built a large brick building which was completed in 1872. The first floor was used as a school and the second floor was for church purposes.

The church building was built in 1883, and dedicated by Archbishop John Ireland in July 1884. In 1908, the parochial school buildings were enlarged and remodeled.

Former pastors of St. Mary's include: the Rev. Aloysius Plut (1865-66), the Rev. J. N. Tomazevic (1866-67), the Rev. William Lette (1867-1871), the Rev. John Schenk (1872-74), the Rev. Sigesbert Mon (1874-79), the Rev. G. Rudolf (1879), the Rev. Joseph Nieblig (1879-80), the Rev. Willibrord Mahowald (1880-1883), the Rev. Alphonse Kuiesle (1883-1895), the Rev. Jerome Heider (1895-1899), the Rev. Pauline Wiesner (1899-1911), the Rev. Conrad Glatzmeier (1911-1919), the Rev. Leonard Kapsner (1919-1923), the Rev. Pius Meinz (1923-1930), the Rev. Robert Wewers (1930-1939), the Rev. Richard Simmer (1939-1940), the Rev. Pius Meinz (1940-1956), the Rev. Oswald Johannes (1956-1959), the Rev. Columban Kremer (1959-1967), the Rev. James Kelly (1967-1968), the Rev. Athanase Fuchs (1968-1971), the Rev. Florian Muggli (1971-1978), the Rev. Thomas Gillespie (1978-1986), the Rev. Vernon Miller (1986-present).

The **Methodist Episcopal Church** was organized by the Rev. Benjamin Close on December 31, 1848, with only eight members.

The first ME Church building was built at a cost of $1,332 and dedicated in November 1854. The Rev. T. M. Fullerton served as the church's pastor until 1860. The Rev. Fullerton also served one year as Stillwater's Mayor. The ME Church was without a regular pastor from 1862 to 1866. In 1866, the Rev. John Stafford took over as pastor and helped guide the membership in the construction of the second church building, which was built in 1869-70. Also, at that

St. Joseph's Catholic Church, Olive and Greeley Streets, ca. 1884.
In May 1883, ten lots were purchased from J. D. McComb to build a church edifice, residence, and school buildings. Early pastors included the Rev. Father J. Eugene Martin, the Rev. A. C. Pettigrew and the Rev. Benjamin Durand. The congregation disbanded in the 1950s.

time, Isaac Staples was on the board of trustees.

The **Swedish Mission Church** was organized by twelve people on September 1, 1881. The first pastor was the Rev. J. W. Carlson. The congregation built a church on North Fourth Street and served them for twenty years. In 1903, it was decided to build a new church and parsonage, which were completed in 1905.

In the 1860s, a Lutheran pastor, the Rev. Hoffman of Lake Elmo, began preaching in Stillwater. About 1869, the Rev. Jacob Siegrist, who succeeded the Rev. Hoffman in Lake Elmo, began the first Lutheran Church in Stillwater. **St. Paul Lutheran Church** (German Lutheran) built a church building and parsonage in 1872, the Rev. Siegrist being its first pastor from 1873 to 1883.

In 1894, the church acquired property on Myrtle and Martha Streets in Stillwater and erected a parish school and teachers home.

Ground breaking for the new St. Paul Lutheran Church were held in October 1950. On February 17, 1951, the farewell service was held in the old church on South Third Street. The first service in the present church building was held the following Sunday. The educational center was built ten years later. The pastors of St. Paul Lutheran after the Rev. Siegrist were: F. Ebert (1889-1903), A. C. Ernst (1904-1947), L. A. Ziemer (1945-1954), R. D. Freseman (1954-1956), Alvin Fritshel (1957-1962), H. P. Senft (1963-1972), Russell J. Quanbeck (1973-1983), and William J. Schonebaum (1984-present).

In 1882 a number of members of the German Lutheran church, in a controversy over predestination, split away from the congregation and on September 12 founded **Salem Lutheran Church**. They purchased the "Swedish Church" at Fourth and Oak Streets. In 1899, the first church was severely damaged by fire. The congregation remodeled what was left and expanded it to provide larger quarters. However, because of the poor location, Salem Lutheran Church built a new building. Ground breaking took place on May 20, 1962 near the south city limits on what is now 62nd Street North. The dedication took place on May 19, 1963.

Trinity Lutheran Church was organized July 18, 1871, with the the Reverend P.A. Cederstam, of Center City, Minnesota, presiding. The formal meeting actually took place the following day, and at that gathering the **Swedish Evangelical Lutheran Church** (Trinity Lutheran) was incorporated and a committee formed to build a church.

The committee purchased the old German Catholic building and an addition was built onto it in 1879. In 1881, the membership had grown to 228, and the congregation decided to purchase two lots on North Third Street for $2,500. In 1883, the church building was built with Andrew Allanson being the contractor.

After the Rev. Cederstam, the Rev. Jonas Ausland served the congregation from 1872-1877; then the Rev. A. F. Tornell (1877-1887); followed by the Rev. Joel L. Haff, (1888-1895); then the Rev. Philip Thelander, (1895-1902); the Rev. A. W. Edwins, (1902-1905); the Rev. C. E. Benson, (1906-1946); the Rev. Norman P. Wold, (1946-1969); the Rev. Forresst E. Chaffee, (1970-1972); and Pastor Daniel Johns (1973-present).

In 1924 the church was renovated with a new addition built to the west to contain the Sacristy, organ and choir room. A new pipe organ also was purchased for the church. In 1933, the membership had grown to 964. In 1948, the congregation purchased land on Fourth Street for a parking area. In 1953, the educational building was completed.

OVERLEAF: Interior of Ascension Episcopal Church, North 3rd Street. ca. 1882, *Frank E. Loomis.*

This original structure was completed in 1875. The church was struck by lightning on Easter 1887 and burned to the ground. The present facility was built on the foundation of the old one year later.

OPPOSITE: Interior of Trinity Swedish Lutheran Church, North 3rd Street. 1901.

St. Paul Lutheran Church, South 3rd Street. ca. 1915, *John Runk Jr.* **German Lutherans attended St. Paulus, known later as St. Paul Evangelical Lutheran Church. This church building located on the west side of 3rd Street near Oak Street was constructed in 1872 and was replaced by the present edifice in 1951.**

In 1982, the congregation authorized construction of new facilities at a cost not to exceed $2.5 million. On October 3, 1982, ground breaking for the building project took place and on May 1, 1983, the last worship was held in the old sanctuary. On March 25, 1984 the first worship service took place in the new sanctuary.

Congregations existing at the turn-of-the-century were: Danish Baptist, First Baptist, St. Joseph's Catholic, St. Mary's Catholic, St. Michael's Catholic, Grace Congregational, Swedish Congregational Mission Church, Ascension Episcopal, German Salem Lutheran, Norwegian Lutheran, St. Ausgar Lutheran, St. Paul Lutheran, St. Peter Lutheran, Swedish Lutheran, 1st Methodist Episcopal, Swedish Methodist Episcopal and 1st Presbyterian.

One hundred fifty years after Stillwater's birth, congregations of the following denominations could be found in Stillwater or in adjacent communities: Apostolic, Assemblies of God, Baptist, Catholic, Charismatic, Christian Science, Episcopal, Evangelical Covenant, Evangelical Free, Interdenominational, Lutheran (ELCA, LCMS, WELS), United Methodist, non-denominational, Presbyterian (USA), Seventh-Day Adventist, United Church of Christ, and Unity.

Argo Bell. 1992, *Brent T. Peterson.*
Today, the Argo bell sits at the Minnesota Historical Society. But in 1846, it sat at the bottom of Lake Pepin. The "Argo" was a steamer that sank and whose bell was salvaged and placed in the school at 4th and Greeley Streets in 1848. The bell rang out throughout the valley and called many children to school until it fell and broke in 1873. After some time, the old bell was given to the historical society.

THERE are many things in this community that residents are proud of, and probably the most is the education that is offered to the youth.

The first school was taught by Sarah L. Judd in 1846. She taught the following year at Point Douglas. Other early school teachers in Stillwater were Mrs. Greenleaf, of Minneapolis, William McKusick, Miss Hosford, and R. B. Johnson in 1849.

In 1850, the organization of the school district under territorial law took place and Stillwater became district one, but later changed to district nine in 1862. In March 1863, the district was organized as the special district of Stillwater.

An election was held in August 1953 for the re-organization of the school districts. Twenty-two districts and parts of others were consolidated to become one large district, which was later numbered 834 by the State Department of Education of Minnesota. District 834 is the largest geographic area in Washington County and stretches from below Afton to a short distance north of Marine-on-St. Croix and is about eight miles wide.

In the spring of 1848, John McKusick gave some lots of land so that a privately funded school house could be built in

Stillwater. School was held in several buildings until John Green and Thomas Sinclair were contracted to build the Central School, which was completed in October 1869. The school cost was $45,000 with twelve rooms, a granite belfry, and steam heat. Also that year, a school was built on North Second Street, called the Schulenberg School, at a cost of $2,700. That, combined with the 70 student capacity of the Central School, quickly filled and another school had to be built just few years later.

In 1873, Lincoln School was built on the corner of North Second and Laurel Streets, called Government Hill. The cost of this 15 room school was also $45,000 but held almost 100 more students. The first day of school was held on September 23, 1874, which included the High School on the third floor. The Lincoln School served Stillwater from that day until September 1939, when demolition workers thought they rang the school's bell for the last time. Today, the bell hangs proudly over the newest Stillwater Area High School, with construction being completed concurrently to this book's publication.

Another School was constructed just two years later, 1875, called the West Primary School, known as the Greeley School,

on South Greeley Street. It held 100 students and cost $4,000 to construct. The Greeley School stood until 1930s, and now private homes stand where the school once did.

In 1887, Stillwater High School was built. No longer did the high school students have to share a building; they had one of their own. This beautiful building served the city of Stillwater until December 23, 1957, when a fire gutted the building.

After 1887, several other schools were built to teach the growing population of Stillwater. The Garfield School was built sometime after the High School and was located on Laurel Street. The capacity of the school was 130 students, and the cost was $6,000. On September 25, 1897, the Nelson School was completed at 1018 South First Street. The total cost being $15,500. After use as a school, Nelson School served as the school district administration building until the early 1970s when a new building was completed on South Greeley Street. Today after refurbishing, the school has been converted into condominiums.

After the turn of the century and the end of logging became a reality in Stillwater, the schools suffered from a lack of financial means. In 1923, Fred M. Tozer made a gift of $75,000 to the school district to be used for

the construction of a gymnasium. When increasing enrollments and an expanded physical education program made enlargement of the gymnasium necessary, the Tozer Foundation made a gift of $150,000 to the district. This gift made possible the expansion of the gymnasium and the installation of a swimming pool.

In 1927, the High School expanded again and added the West Wing. Then in 1939, the East Wing was constructed directly across Third Street, which would serve as Stillwater Junior High School. Also in 1939, the Washington School was completed and used as an Elementary school, and most recently, used as an extension of the High School.

After the High School fire of 1957, high school students were placed in several schools until a new high school building was built. That building was completed in 1960. Rising student populations created a need for expansion, but no room or acceptable plan could be found. So in the mid-1970s the district initiated a four-day-a-week plan so that the students could fit in the building. Another plan was to rent space in another school in St. Paul named Hillside. After the attendance came down in the mid-1980s, Hillside was discarded and all stu-

OPPOSITE: Lincoln School, School Street. ca. 1909, *John Runk Jr.*
Lincoln School was built on McKusick's old burying grounds on the North Hill. Runk likely attended this school. It served as Stillwater High School prior to the completion of the 1888 building at Pine & 3rd Streets. Lincoln School's bell is now being used in the 1993-completed high school.

Maude E. Soule. ca. 1883, *John M. Kuhn.*
Maude was a school teacher at both the Lincoln and Greeley schools.

Stillwater High School, Pine and 3rd Streets. 1934, *A. Pearson Company.*
The original building to the right was destroyed by fire in 1957. The remaining two buildings which were added in the 1920s and 1930s became part of Stillwater Junior High School in 1960 when a new high school was completed. A tunnel under 3rd Street linked the east and west wings.

OPPOSITE: Stillwater Area High School, Trunk Highway 5. October 1992, *Brent T. Peterson.*
The new high school is getting the finishing touches, including the old Lincoln School Bell, high above the administration section.

dents remained in the district starting in 1985. So now, the district is completing construction of a new High School building just south of highway 36, to be opened in the sesquicentennial year. The old Senior High School building will become the new home of the Stillwater Junior High, and the old Junior High building will either be torn down or made into office space.

In 1964, Lily Lake Elementary was built near the shores of Lily Lake. To provide a nearby school for the north part of town, Stonebridge Elementary was completed on North Owens Street in 1971. On the south edge of town is Oak Park Elementary, a school for children who live in Stillwater and Oak Park Heights.

The German Catholic school was organized in 1871, and a building was erected soon after, on fifth Street, between Pine and Oak Streets. The entire cost of the site, building, sister's house and furniture, was about $12,000.

A German School was organized in the spring of 1873, at the German Lutheran Church on Third Street, between Oak and Olive Streets. It started with forty students, and the first instructor was the Rev. Jacob Siegrist.

1865

Main Street

1872

1888

1992

JACOB FISHER

Mr. Fisher was born in Canada on November 30, 1813. He arrived to work at the mill at St. Croix Falls, Wisconsin Territory in 1842.

His vocation was as a millwright and carpenter, and he helped build most of the early sawmills on the St. Croix River.

He spent the winter of 1842-43 at "Dakotah," a trading post at the head of Lake St. Croix. After discovering an excellent location for another sawmill nearby, he claimed the land. This claim later became the site of Stillwater Lumber Company and town of the same name.

On January 4, 1862, Fisher enlisted into the Union Army and was the wagoner of the Second Company of Sharpshooters. He was wounded at the battle of Cold Harbor, Virginia and was discharged from Company A, 1st Minnesota Battalion on June 26, 1865.

On April 9, 1889, he was committed to the Rochester Hospital for the Insane and passed away five days later, April 14, 1889, of heart disease.

GEORGE H. SULLIVAN

Mr. Sullivan was born is Stillwater on December 20, 1867. He was educated in the city's schools and was graduated from the University of Wisconsin Law School on June 20, 1888.

Sullivan was elected to the Minnesota State Senate in 1906, and served in that body until his death with the exception of 1916 & 1917 when he served as Minnesota's Lt. Governor. He held the chairmanship of the Senate Tax Committee; he was the president of the National Association of States on Bank Taxes. He campaigned for national banking levies and was frequently called to Washington, D. C. for consultation.

In 1904, Sullivan was named a member of the Republican State Central Committee and served on that board for several years.

He was married to Kittie Brand, of Madison, Wisconsin in 1888. Together they had one daughter and two sons.

George H. Sullivan passed away at his home in Mahtomedi, Minnesota on February 15, 1935.

Lt. Governor George H. Sullivan (1867-1935) ca. 1912.

Samuel Bloomer (1835-1917)
ca. 1881, *John M. Kuhn*

SAMUEL BLOOMER

Samuel Bloomer was born at Engi Canton, Glarus, Switzerland on November 30, 1835. He came to the United States with his parents in 1846 and settled in St. Louis. After two years there, the Bloomers moved to Stillwater, Minnesota.

In 1861, when the Civil War broke out, Samuel Bloomer enlisted in Company B, First Minnesota Regiment. He was detailed as one of the color guards on June 3, 1862, after the battle of Fair Oaks. He was promoted from orporal to color sergeant and carried the colors of the regiment through the following engagements: Savage Station, Glendale, White Oak Swamp, Malvern Hill, South Mountain, and Antietam. He was wounded twice during the war: once at the first battle of Bull Run when a bullet grazed his head, and again at the battle of Antietam, in which he lost his leg. After the wound he suffered at Antietam, Bloomer was discharged on December 6, 1862. On August 1, 1863, President Lincoln appointed him lieutenant in the Veterans Reserve Corps, in which he served until discharged on September 19, 1866.

Sam Bloomer was married in Evansville, Indiana on December 12, 1863, and had four children: Alice, Charles, Grace, and Ernest. Bloomer again married on October 7, 1882 to Nellie Presnell.

In 1888, he was elected County Treasurer, an office he held for six years.

On June 14, 1905, Sam Bloomer once again carried the colors of the First Minnesota Regiment, this time from the old capitol building to the new one on Constitution Avenue in St. Paul. It and other significant flags in Minnesota history remain on display in the rotunda.

On October 4, 1917, Stillwater's bravest soldier, Samuel Bloomer, died at his home in Mahtomedi, at the age of 82. He was a member of the Grand Army of the Republic, the Military Order of the Loyal Legion of the United States, and the local lodge of the Knights of Pythias.

In 1992, seventy-five years after his death, a flag pole was dedicated in Bloomer's honor at Fort Ripley, Minnesota.

ROY G. STAPLES

Mr. Staples was born on April 22, 1873, the son of Samuel and Mary (Wilson) Staples. At the age of seven, Roy's father died, and the family moved to Anoka, Minnesota. After graduating from high school there, Staples enlisted in Company K, First Minnesota Regiment on May 14, 1890 at Stillwater, Minnesota. He was promoted many times and became a first lieutenant on May 24, 1895. On April 29, 1898, Staples enrolled in the 14th Minnesota Infantry Volunteers for service in the Spanish-American War. He was discharged on November 10, 1898.

Staples married Clementine Reed, daughter of William Reed, in 1907. They had

Roy G. Staples (1873-1931)
ca. 1925.

two children: a daughter, Eleanor, and a son, Wilson.

Staples was the President of the Cosmopolitan State Bank of Stillwater, Treasurer of the Washington County Building-Loan Association, Manager of the Stillwater Insurance Agency, Secretary of the Lowell Inn Hotel Company. In 1900, Staples was appointed postmaster at Maple Island, Washington County, Minnesota. He also served as an officer of the Western Shoe Company and became vice president of the Gotzian Shoe Company in St. Paul, Minnesota.

Roy G. Staples, grand-nephew to Isaac Staples, passed away quietly at his home in Stillwater at 212 Cherry Street on October 30, 1931.

JOHN C. NETHAWAY

Nethaway was born in Albany, New York on November 12, 1857. He came to Stillwater about the year 1880, and proceeded to practice law.

He served, respectively, as judge of the municipal court of Stillwater, county attorney and assistant to the Attorney General of Minnesota. Nethaway was appointed judge of the Nineteenth Judicial District, in January 1916, by Governor Burnquist, and was elected for the full term of six years the following fall.

Nethaway was married on June 18, 1885, to Cora Hall. The couple had two sons, Clinton and Gullford.

Judge Nethaway was a charter member of the Stillwater Elks Lodge, No. 179, a

Hon. Judge John C. Nethaway (1857-1917)
ca. 1912

member of the Maccabees and of the Modern Woodmen.

J. C. Nethaway passed away in Shakopee, Minnesota, where he went to take "baths" for his rheumatic trouble. Nethaway had a fainting spell and died a couple hours later, on July 4, 1917.

Edwin D. Buffington (1858-1931)
ca. 1915

EDWIN D. BUFFINGTON

Buffington was born at Warren, Pennsylvania on October 6, 1858. At a very young age he, along with his family, moved to Towanda, Pennsylvania and it was there that he attended public schools. He later was graduated from the Susquehanna Collegiate Institute.

He studied law with the firm of Williams and Angie in Towanda and was admitted to the bar there. He came to Stillwater in 1881 and worked in the legal department of the Northwestern Manufacturing Company. Later he became general manager and secretary of the Minnesota Thresher Manufacturing Company which became the Northwest Thresher Company. In 1893, Buffington was appointed receiver of the Stillwater Union Depot & Transfer Company.

He formed the law partnership of Buffington & Buffington with his brother in Minneapolis. Edwin later returned to Stillwater and practised law until Buffington became Stillwater's City Attorney on April 12, 1911 and served in that position also until he died.

He was married in New York City to Sarah K. Kinney on March 16, 1881. The couple only had one child, a son.

He was a member of the American Bar Association; Minnesota State Bar Association, of which he was a member of the board of governors; the Nineteenth Judicial District Bar Association, of which he served as President in 1928; and Washington County Bar Association.

Edwin D. Buffington passed away at the home of T. R. Converse on January 26, 1931.

JAY A. GOGGIN

Mr. Goggin was born in Oak Park on March 12, 1899, the son of Mr. and Mrs. James Goggin. Jay received his secondary education from the Stillwater area schools.

On November 23, 1925, Goggin was united in marriage with Viola Diestler, in Aberdeen, South Dakota. The two had one son, Jerry, and one daughter, Mary (Frazier).

In 1935, J. A. Goggin purchased the Starkel Candy Company from Nick Starkel. Goggin ran the company under the same name until 1940, when he renamed it to the Goggin Candy Company. He started with only four employees, but by the end of one year, he had twenty-seven people producing Goggin candies. Goggin's Candy closed on February 15, 1989.

Goggin was a director of the Farmers and Merchants State Bank in Stillwater, a past President of the Stillwater Rotary club, a past Exulted Ruler of the Stillwater Elks

Lodge No. 179, and a past member of the Stillwater Masonic Lodge No. 1.

Jay A. Goggin passed away in Stillwater on August 18, 1963.

ELMORE LOWELL

Lowell was born on January 20, 1851 in Concord, Maine, the son of Albert and Abbie Lowell. He came to Stillwater when three years old and received his education through the public schools of Stillwater. He followed his father in the hotel business, taking over the Sawyer House after his father's death. The Sawyer House became very popular under Elmore's direction, and it was during this time that the Civil War veterans formed the Last Man's Club at the Sawyer House. He brought dignity to not only the hotel, but also to the City of Stillwater. Elmore Lowell retired from the hotel business in 1902, and traveled to many parts of the world.

In 1910, when the city was raising funds to develop the river front, Elmore Lowell made the largest contribution to the project, hence the name Lowell Park. He also served several years as one of the park commissioners of Stillwater and as chairman of that board.

For his kindness and contributions to the City of Stillwater, Elmore Lowell was the first inductee into Stillwater's Hall of Fame established in 1931.

By 1935, Lowell had moved to Los Angeles, California to live with his brother Charles A. Lowell. On a short walk, Elmore fell and broke his hip, which placed him in a hospital. Mr. Lowell died several days later at the age of 83.

JOHN R. STOLTZE

Stoltze was born in St. Paul, Minnesota, attended St. Paul Academy, then Hill School in Pottstown, Pennsylvania. He was graduated from Princeton University in 1917. He was 2nd Lieutenant in the Army in World War I. In 1920 he went to Shreveport, Louisiana, leasing and promoting oil land. Later he became sales and traffic manager for Crystal Oil & Refining Co., of Shreveport. In 1928 he went to Minneapolis to join his father in operating lumber yards in Saskatchewan, Canada.

Upon the death of his father in 1929, he took over the business and continued its operation. He traded his Minneapolis home

Elmore Lowell (1851-1935)
ca. 1869

Charles Jackson (1851-1903) and his dog King. 1892, *Edward Johnson*.

for Maple Island Farm north of Stillwater in 1933, where he raised hogs and dairy cattle. He eventually specialized on the dairy herd and marketing milk. He established a pasteurizing plant and later a milk drying plant from which grew the Maple Island, Inc. powdered whole milk operation.

Stoltze served several terms as chairman of the board of Summit School from 1934 to 1957. He was a charter member of the St. Paul Chamber Orchestra and a supporter of the Minnesota Bach Society.

John R. Stoltze died at his home in Afton, Minnesota on January 16, 1991, at the age of 95.

CHARLES JACKSON

Jackson was born outside of Atlanta, Georgia about the year 1851. Like most other blacks at that time, he was born into slavery.

In October, 1864, a raiding party from the 101st Indiana Regiment invaded the plantation on which Jackson lived. He helped the regiment secure all that was usable, and followed the Indiana Regiment to Atlanta in time to see the city burn.

Jackson soon took ill and was placed in a hospital to recover. During that time the Indiana Regiment went north. Charles Jackson followed as soon as he was well enough to travel, and caught the Regiment just outside Washington, D. C. The 101st Indiana Regiment, along with Charles Jackson, met up with the 2nd Minnesota Regiment in Pittsburgh, Pennsylvania. Jackson then followed the Minnesota regiment back to Fort Snelling in Minnesota, where he worked for E. B. Whitcher at St. Paul.

Jackson became acquainted with Albert Lowell who ran the Sawyer House hotel in Stillwater. Lowell told Jackson that if he ever needed a job there was one waiting for him in Stillwater. Jackson, after not being paid promised wages from Whitcher, set out for Stillwater with only ten cents in his pocket.

Jackson took up the barber trade, becoming one of the most liked barbers in Stillwater, eventually heading out on his own. For a time, he teamed up with another black barber named Sam Hadley, forming the tonsorial partnership of Hadley & Jackson.

Jackson married Mattie Porter in 1871.

Charles Jackson, a one time slave that became a well-known businessman in Stillwater, passed away at his home on Churchill Street in Stillwater on May 5, 1903. On that day, in honor of Charles Jackson, all barbershops were closed in Stillwater.

ELAM GREELEY

Elam Greeley was born at Salisbury, New Hampshire on August 13, 1818. When he was about eight years old, he moved with his family to Maine. In 1839, he traveled to Rockford, Illinois then on to Prairie Du Chien, Wisconsin then to Chippewa Falls, Wisconsin. In the same year he met John McKusick. They traveled to St. Croix Falls and organized a lumber company. In 1843, Greeley, McKusick, and others built a saw mill in what is now Stillwater. After one year, Greeley sold his interest in the mill and devoted his occupation to lumbering, rafting, and shipping of logs.

On August 25, 1850, Greeley married Hannah P. Hinman, and they had five children: Phoebe, Judson H., Kate, Douglas, and John E..

Elam Greeley was the first postmaster in Stillwater, he also was elected to the upper house of the third territorial legislature in 1852, and elected to the lower house in 1857.

On September 13, 1882, Greeley was in Cumberland, Wisconsin. While setting a brake on a railroad flat car, he suffered an attack of paralysis and fell to the ground, breaking his shoulder. His son Douglas ran to his side, but Elam was unconscious and passed away four hours later. Elam Greeley's body was transported back to Stillwater several days later. The funeral took place at the family home at the corner of Myrtle and Greeley Streets.

JOSEPH WOLF

Wolf was born in Truns, Switzerland on January 4, 1832. He came to Stillwater in 1855 bringing with him a small amount of baggage, and nothing else except good health, a brave heart and willing hands.

Wolf first started working in the lumber industry, then in 1871 he engaged in the brewing business with the firm Wolf, Tanner & Company. In 1880, the firm was dissolved and Joseph Wolf took entire control. In 1896, Wolf incorporated his business to include his three sons and two sons-in-law.

He was married to Anna Mary Simonet on August 10, 1858. They renewed their vows 50 years later and were able to enjoy a 62nd wedding anniversary. They parented 14 children.

In 1911, Wolf erected the Wolf Building on the site of McKusick's old store. For many years the Grand Cafe was located there and today Images of the Past and Present is located within the building.

Joseph Wolf, Sr. (1832-1921) ca. 1899, *Emil Okerblad.*

Wolf took ill suddenly and died on May 27, 1921 at his home and business at 402 South Main Street. Today it is Vittorio's restaurant.

(L-R): Louis J. Kuhn (1869-1946),
John M. Kuhn (1855-1910).
ca. 1897, *John M. Kuhn.*

JOHN M. KUHN

John M. Kuhn came to Stillwater in 1882, taking over the well-established photography business of James Sinclair at 109 South Main Street. For many years Kuhn was the best known photographic artist in the city. He took many stereo views of Stillwater and received photo orders from many organizations such as the Holman English Opera Company.

In 1889, Kuhn's brother, Louis joined him in the photography business in Stillwater. In 1897, the Kuhn Brothers moved to St. Paul. About 1903, Louis re-established a shop in Stillwater. The St. Paul studio closed in 1908.

After the St. Paul shop closed, John moved his studio west, and it was in Anaheim, California where the photographer passed away on July 26, 1910 at the age of 55. He was a member of the Masonic Order, had taken the Scottish Rite, and was a Noble of Osman Temple Shriners. He was also a member of the Elks, Modern Woodmen, and Ancient Order of United Workmen. He was also one of the original members of Company K, which was organized on April 5, 1883.

LOUIS J. KUHN

Mr. Kuhn was born at Columbus, Ohio on November 16, 1869. He was educated in the public schools in Columbus. His first job was with Wells Tracy & Company wholesale drug store in Columbus.

In 1889, he came to Stillwater and joined his brother, John M. Kuhn, in the photography business. Louis left Stillwater for a few years, but returned about 1903 with his own shop at 123 East Chestnut Street. During this time the Kuhns operated galleries in both Stillwater and St. Paul, but in 1908, the St. Paul gallery closed, and the brothers went their separate ways. Not long after, Louis went back to 109 South Main.

On June 27, 1900, Louis Kuhn married Mary Eliza Goodrich, the daughter of Mr. and Mrs. John Goodrich, of Stillwater.

Kuhn was a member of the Royal Arcanum, and Ancient Order of United Workmen. He died in Stillwater in 1946.

Victor Carlton Seward (1845-1892)
1892.

VICTOR C. SEWARD

Mr. Seward was born in Laketon, Indiana, on July 10, 1845, and when he was ten years of age, moved with his family to Mankato, Minnesota. He was graduated from the Western Reserve College in Hudson. He returned to St. Paul, Minnesota in 1868 and worked with the St. Paul *Dispatch* newspaper. In 1869 he started the Redwood Falls *Mail* newspaper, which he abandoned in 1873. He then joined with his brother-in-law, S. S. Taylor, and bought the Stillwater *Messenger.* Seward became the sole owner of the *Messenger* upon Taylor's death in the 1880s.

Victor Seward was married to Lizzie Putman in 1871. Together they had a daughter named Mable.

On Tuesday, October 11, 1892, Victor Seward was assassinated by a former employee of the *Messenger,* George Peters. Peters was hired to be a reporter, but the young Peters could not perform the job. Seward was patient with Peters but then suggested to him that he find another vocation. With that, Peters swore vengeance on Victor Seward for firing him. Nobody took the threat for real, and at about five in the afternoon on October 11, 1892, Peters returned to Seward's office. George Peters did not find Seward there so he went into Stillwater to find him. It was not long before Peters found Seward walking on Main Street. Peters shouted at Seward, and when Seward turned around, Peters shot him in the head. Seward staggered into the doorway of Drechsler's Music Store. Peters followed him and fired twice more into Seward's head, killing him instantly.

EDWARD WHITE DURANT

Durant was born in Roxbury, Massachusetts on April 8, 1829. At the age of two he moved with his family to Cincinnati and later to Illinois where his boyhood was passed as a frontier farmer.

In April, 1848, at the age of 19, Durant moved to Stillwater and engaged in the lumber industry. He was a rafter on the river for three years then piloted river boats for several more years. He, with partners R. J. Wheeler and A. T. Jenks, built and ran steamboats between Stillwater and St. Louis under the firm of Durant, Wheeler and Company.

Durant was appointed Mayor of Stillwater in 1861, and later served three more terms in that office. He was elected

Edward White Durant (1829-1918)
1887, *C. A. Zimmerman,* St. Paul, Minnesota.

to three terms in both the Senate and House of Representatives in Minnesota and was the Democratic candidate for Lt. Governor of Minnesota and for U.S. Senator.

He was married to Henrietta Pease on December 29, 1853. The couple had two daughters and one son.

Durant was a Mason of the St. John's Lodge No. 1 of Stillwater and was elected

Oscar Ostrom (1863-1937)
1937, *Louis Kuhn.*

Grand Master of Masons in Minnesota in 1878. He was also elected Grand Chancellor of Knights of Pythias of Minnesota in 1874.

Edward White Durant died at the home of his daughter in Stillwater on Sunday December 9, 1918 at the age of 89.

OSCAR OSTROM

Mr. Ostrom was born in Wexio, Sweden on July 20, 1863 and came to this country and Stillwater in 1881. He worked in the lumber business eleven years. In 1892, Ostrom married Alice Peterson and together they took charge of the East Side Lumber Company's Boarding House. Also in 1892, he had a financial interest in the "Vienna Restaurant" as a partner in Ostrom & Swanson.

In 1902, Ostrom was elected Sheriff of Washington County and served in that capacity until 1910. In 1911, he took control of the Sawyer House, the largest and most notable hotel in Stillwater, and ran the hotel until 1924 when it was torn down to make way for the Lowell Inn. After the Sawyer House, Ostrom owned and operated the Grand Cafe.

Ostrom died on May 29, 1937 at the age of 73.

ALPHEUS KINGSLEY DOE

A. K. "King" Doe was born in 1837 in Oldtown, Maine. He came to Stillwater when he was about twenty years of age. He first found employment with Isaac Staples. He later became a partner in such companies as Hersey, Staples & Doe; Hersey & Doe; Staples, Doe & Hersey; Hersey, Bronson, Doe & Folsom. Doe later became the manager of the Stillwater Hardware Company. Later he became owner and manager of the Sawyer House.

"King" Doe was elected Stillwater City Treasurer in 1863, elected recorder in 1866, and then elected Stillwater Mayor in 1873. In 1892, he was elected Clerk of Court, an office he held until January 1905.

On June 20, 1907, A. K. Doe died at the Stillwater City Hospital at 10:10 A.M. Mr. Doe had four sons: F. P. Doe; D. H. Doe, R. H. Doe; and Judge Alpheus Edwin Doe.

WILLIAM WILLIM

William Willim was born in Woolhope, County of Hereford, England, on June 26, 1821. He came to the United States in 1837 and to Stillwater in 1844.

In 1847, Mr. Willim was married to Clara G. Haskell who died a short time later. He remarried in 1856 to Joanna W. Hinman. The couple had three children: Mrs. George S. Millard, William B., and Myron S.. The second Mrs. Willim died in 1884.

William Willim was issued the first naturalization document in Minnesota. The document has the date of June 18, 1847, at Stillwater, St. Croix County, Wisconsin Territory and is signed by Joseph R. Brown.

Willim was a contractor and builder by trade and built some of the first buildings in Stillwater. He was a member of the sixth Minnesota Territorial Legislature and served as mayor in 1856, 1866, and 1867. He was a member of the Old Settler's Association, and was the president of that association when he passed away, February 22, 1895.

LOUISE M. (JARCHOW) JOHNSON

Mrs. Johnson was born in Stillwater on April 16, 1905. She attended local schools and was graduated from Stillwater High School in 1923. She was honored with the school's Distinguished Alumnus Award in 1990.

She was graduated from the University of Minnesota in 1927 and taught high school math and English for 17 years: three years at Hutchinson, Minnesota and fourteen at Willow River, Minnesota.

Mrs. Johnson began the public health nursing service in Pine County in 1937 and served as Willow River health officer and chairperson of the board of health until 1952, when she and her husband Herbert and their two children moved to Stillwater.

She helped start the home-delivered meals program in Washington County, helped organize the Senior Citizen drop-in center, was the curator of the Washington County Historical Museum in Stillwater. She lead the "save the courthouse" fund drive along with many other community projects.

Mrs. Johnson was named Outstanding Senior Citizen in Washington County in 1973; was named the local BPW Chapter Woman of the Year in 1976; was awarded the 1983-84 Stillwater Jaycee's Karl Neumeier Award for continued contributions to the community; was honored by the AAUW with a scholarship awarded in her name to promote higher education; and was the recipient of WCCO Radio's Good Neighbor Award on three occasions.

Louise M. Johnson passed away at the Greeley Healthcare Center in Stillwater on December 8, 1991.

Louise M. Johnson (1905-1991) 1970.

THOMAS W. CURTIS

Curtis was born in Stillwater on September 16, 1892.

In 1932, Curtis started a feed, seed, fuel, and farm equipment business in Stillwater in the building that is now the Freight House restaurant.

In the mid-1930s, he was instrumental in organizing the Farmer's Buying Association and served several terms as the association's president. He was also the director of the Twin Cities Milk Producers Association and played an active role in drawing attention to the farmers' plight.

Curtis purchased the old Wolf Brewery in 1945. He converted the upper level into apartments and in the lower portion, he and a partner had a DeSoto car agency. Curtis later purchased the entire business and then rented the agency to another dealer. He is probably best known for opening one of the first tourist attractions in Stillwater, Curtis Caves.

The Caves were used originally to store and age the kegs of Wolf's beer, but Curtis added trout ponds and opened them to the public for a small fee. Thousands of tourist went through the caves from the late 1950s until Curtis sold them in 1971.

Thomas W. Curtis (1892-1985)
ca. 1970, *A. Pearson Company*.

Tom Curtis also wrote about Stillwater and its history in the Stillwater Gazette. He is remembered in Stillwater for his outspoken opinions and his love for Stillwater. Mr. Curtis died at the Linden Health Care Center on April 4, 1985, at the age of 92.

JOHN GREEN

John Green was born in Ireland on March 1, 1818. He came to Charlottetown, Edwards Valley, in the Gulf of St. Lawrence in 1836. He moved to Boston, Massachusetts two years later, then to New York City in 1840. He went from there to Ohio and Alabama, settling in Stillwater just after the Civil War in 1866.

He was a builder and contractor and became highly successful in Stillwater, building many important structures of the day.

He was married in 1838 to M. J. Pinkerton. The couple had four children: John R., Frank, Jennie, and Agnes. After the death of his wife, John Green left Stillwater and resided in Gladstone, Michigan. John Green passed away on March 15, 1896 in Gladstone, Michigan and was buried in Stillwater, Minnesota.

ABRAM HALL

Mr. Hall was born in Luzerne County, Pennsylvania on February 8, 1835. He went to school in Bradford County until the age of fourteen. His father then taught him the clothing business. Abe worked with his father for the next five years. He then moved to Wilkesbarre, Pennsylvania and remained there for two years. In 1858, Abe moved to Waupun, Wisconsin where he became the Yardmaster at the Wisconsin State Prison. He worked at the prison until 1864, when he quit and started working in the hotel business in Waupun. He left Waupun in 1867 and settled in Stillwater, Minnesota in 1868, and was employed at the Minnesota State Prison. In 1876, Abe Hall was commissioned as deputy warden and served in that position until his death.

Abe Hall married Letta Ames while at Waupun, Wisconsin in 1861. The couple had two daughters, Cora, who married Judge John C. Nethaway, and Eva. Abe Hall died of tuberculosis on July 28, 1886.

DWIGHT M. SABIN

Mr. Sabin was born at Marseilles, Illinois on April 25, 1843. In 1856, because of his father's illness, the Sabin's moved to Connecticut. Several years later, the family settled in Killingly, Connecticut until his father died in 1864. In 1867, Dwight, his younger brother Jay, and their mother, moved to Minnesota. They settled in Stillwater one year later.

The Sabins formed the firm of Seymour, Sabin & Company with Dwight Sabin as president of the firm. This company later merged into the Northwestern Manufacturing and Car Company, which failed in 1884. Sabin also owned a one-half interest in the milling and elevator firm of J. H. Townshend & Company, the Chicago Railway and Equipment Company, and other large businesses throughout the West.

In 1882, Dwight Sabin was elected to the United States Senate over William Windom. He served until 1889, when he was defeated in his bid for re-election by W. D. Washburn. He also served in both houses of the state Legislature and as a delegate to several national Republican Conventions.

While spending the winter in Chicago, Dwight M. Sabin died on December 23, 1902.

Dwight M. Sabin (1843-1902)
1882.

James A. Mulvey (1835-1910)
ca. 1865.

JAMES A. MULVEY

Mulvey was born at Cranbrook, Kent County, England on March 25, 1835. At thirteen he moved to the United States and settled with his family in New York State.

In May 1853, Mulvey moved to Stillwater and became involved in the lumber industry. Nine years later, he enlisted in Company C., Eighth Minnesota Infantry and served until his discharge on July 11, 1865.

On October 26, 1865, Mulvey married Miranda Edwards of Stillwater, and to them were born four children: Arthur J., Jesse A., Edna M., and Walter S.

After the Civil War, Mulvey went back to the lumber business. In the winter of 1880-81, he banked over two million feet of logs. James Mulvey also helped start the Clearwater Logging Company, along with William O'Brien of St. Paul, and Otis Staples of Stillwater, in September 1897.

Mulvey was a member of the Presbyterian Church and served as president of its board of trustees for many years. He also was a charter member and commander of G.A.R. Post No. 69.

James Mulvey died at his home on Churchill Street, which is now a bed and breakfast, on July 13, 1910.

BYRON J. MOSIER

Mosier was born in Walworth, New York on June 29, 1847. Mosier attended school only in the winter when a young child. In the summer he worked on neighboring farms. When he was 17 years old, he enlisted in Company H, 194th Volunteer Infantry of New York and attained the rank of corporal by the end of the Civil War.

In 1866, he moved to Michigan then on to Stillwater, Minnesota in 1871. He was in the painting business for ten years and in 1882, he formed a partnership with his brother, Charles E. Mosier, in a retail and wholesale tobacco business. Also that year, the Mosiers took in a "silent partner," a 350- pound wooden Indian.

Minnesota's Governor John Lind appointed Mosier Surveyor General of Logs and Lumber of the First District of Minnesota. Mosier was an unsuccessful candidate for State Treasurer in 1905. Mosier was elected to the Stillwater City Council in 1909 and later served two years as Stillwater's Mayor, in 1912-13.

Mosier was married to Clara A. Mason at Ottawa, Illinois on January 8, 1871. The couple had three children: Mrs. John A. McPike; Mrs. Margie McMillan; and E. M. Mosier.

Bryon J. Mosier passed away on Sunday January 22, 1933. He was a commander of Stillwater Post No. 1, G.A.R.. He was the president of the board of trustees and also served as adjutant of the Soldiers Home from 1925 until his death. He was a charter member of the Stillwater Lodge of Elks, a member of Knights Templar and the Shrine Lodge. He was a member of the Sons of the American Revolution.

ERLE J. (BABE) ORFF

Orff was born in Stillwater on March 19, 1917. He attended local schools and was graduated from Stillwater High School in 1934.

As a youngster, Orff caddied at a golf course near his home. He caddied often for a man named Dan McCush, who thought enough of Orff's golf talent that he sponsored him in several tournaments. When Orff got out of the Army after World War II, he applied for and became the pro at the Stillwater Country Club, a position he held until he retired in 1981.

He was married to his wife Helen on April 28, 1940. The couple had three children: Judd, Debbie (Nelson), and Maureen (Paulson).

Erle J. "Babe" Orff passed away after playing eighteen holes of golf at Myrtle Beach, South Carolina on February 25, 1991.

JASPER NEWTON SEARLES

Mr. Searles was born in North Royalton, Ohio on November 9, 1840. He came with his parents to Minnesota in 1855 settling in Hastings. Searles enlisted into Company H, First Minnesota Regiment as a private in 1861. He was later made second and first lieutenant of companies H and G and finally captain of Company C of the First Minnesota Regiment. He was discharged in 1864.

In 1866, Searles entered the law school of the University of Michigan, earning his LL.B. in 1869. Also in 1866, Searles Married Sara Lewis Tozer; they had three children together. He first practised law in Hastings, but moved to Stillwater in 1881. After many years of practice in Stillwater, Searles was appointed Judge of the 19th Judicial District of Minnesota in 1917 by Governor Burnquist; he was elected to that position in 1918, serving until January 1925.

Judge Jasper N. Searles died at his home in Stillwater on April 25, 1927.

Hon. Judge Jasper Newton Searles (1840-1927) ca. 1863.

9 Acknowledgements, Photo Credits and Bibliography

IT is our hope that Stillwater's history is told in a special way in these pages. With the great photographs held in the collections of our local libraries and historical societies, we knew that the most important part of Stillwater's story was told in pictures.

It was our intent to focus entirely on Stillwater subjects. Only a handful of the photographs were taken outside of the city limits.

Interestingly, we only had to dip into the John Runk Historical Collection one time for a photo of James A. Mulvey. John Runk knew the importance of photographs to St. Croix Valley history. Taken by many different photographers, less than half of the collection's prints are of his own making. Beginning in 1936, he presented parts of this special collection of 600 photograph reproductions to four differ-

ent groups: Minnesota Historical Society, Stillwater Public Library, Washington County Historical Society and St. Croix County Historical Society. After Runk's death in 1964, The Minnesota Historical Society was given a series of original Runk negatives, prints and motion picture films which represent the bulk of his creativity.

Most of the photos are from the collections of the Washington County Historical Society. We found a great number of school and business photos perfect for the scope of this book and we gratefully acknowledge the society for allowing us to bring in computer equipment and digitally scan the photographs on-site.

We also were able to locate some special Stillwater photographs in the collections of the Minnesota Historical Society. During the years

we put this book together we followed the collection during its move into the Minnesota History Center, an excellent research and display facility worthy of our Minnesota past. A few of these photos were located among thousands of newspaper negatives. These photos were printed once and have now been printed again for our lasting pleasure. We thank the St. Paul *Dispatch* and *Pioneer Press* photographers who made the trip out to Stillwater and helped preserve our past.

Photographers

To aid in the identification of your own Stillwater photographs, we provide the following list of professional Stillwater area photographers and the approximate dates that they were in business:

Anderson, Jack M. ....ca. 1947-1971
Andrews, A. W. ....ca. 1871-1872
Carli, Christopher H. .....ca. 1870-1878
Chetlain, C. E. & B. Truaisch .ca. 1859
Chial, Debra ....ca. 1985-present
Colonial Studios ....ca. 1965-66
Cooper, Herbert D. ....ca. 1904-1907
Dellarson Studios ....ca. 1982-1984
Donald, Jeremiah ....ca. 1888-1891
Edwards, L. E. ....ca. 1906
Empire Portrait Studios ....ca. 1947
Ermisch, Carl R. ....ca. 1944-1951
Everitt, E. F. ....ca. 1864-1866
Foley, John S. ....ca. 1887-93
Halmrast Bros. ....ca. 1893-1896
Halmrast, Gustav ....ca. 1896-1919
Hamilton, Grant C. ....ca. 1866
Hansen Studios ....ca. 1926-1932

Johnson, Edward .... ca. 1893-1896
Judd, Sarah L. .... ca. 1848-1850
Kuhn, John M. .... ca. 1882-1897
Kuhn, Louis J. .... ca. 1903-1943
Larson, L. C. .... ca. 1898-1901
Leander, Carl A. .... ca. 1904-1906
Lee, Bruce .... ca. 1986-1988
Loomis, Frank E. .... ca. 1877-1882
Loomis, Frank E. & W. H. Loofborrow
.... ca. 1882-83
Main Street Studio .... ca. 1979-1981
Moore, G. W. .... ca. 1883-1885
Okerblad, Emil .... ca. 1898-1903
Oleson, E. .... ca. 1887
Peirce, E. W. & B. F. Fuller 1859
Portraits by Loren ..... ca. 1987-present
Portraits by Miles .... ca. 1976-1989
Runk, John .... ca. 1899-1964
Sargent, F. H. .... ca. 1897-1904
Scherling Pletsch Studiosca. 1972-1974
Silver Light Studio .... ca. 1982-present
Sinclair, R. H. & Brother 1866-1871
Sinclair, James 1871-1882
Stridborg, J. A. .... ca. 1876-1877
Stridborg & Loomis 1877
Sunrise Studio .... ca. 1981-1985
Tiny Tot Photo .... ca. 1962
Valley Photo & Music Shop . ca. 1967-
    1969
Van Buskirk, James .... ca. 1880-1882
Van Zee, Ron M. ...... ca. 1977-present
Wenzin, John .... ca. 1856
Wiklund, Laurentz .... ca. 1883-1893
Wolff Photo .... ca. 1977
Wolff, Russell J. .... ca. 1965-66
Wolff, Russell J. & Associatesca. 1969-
    1970

We'd like to thank...

Ascension Episcopal Church
Lee Bjerk, Images of the Past and Present
Sue Collins, St. Croix Collection, Stillwater Public Library
Mark Crimmins
Ruby Crotto
Joan Daniels, Curator, Warden's House Museum, Washington County Historical Society
Chuck and Judy Dougherty
Catherine Flynn
Terry Giebler
Glenn Goggin & Richard Schell
Jim Johnson
Rosa Bailey Jones
Carol Maki
Lee Ostrom, *Courier News*
Frank and Evelyn Peterson
Roger and Darlene Peterson
St. Paul Lutheran Church
Mrs. Wilson Staples
Allen and Janet Stevens
Trinity Lutheran Church
Bonnie Wilson, Audio-Visual Collection, Minnesota Historical Society
Marlene Workman-DeBoef, Washington County Historic Courthouse
Peter Zang

Photo Credits

Original photographer or publisher, if known, is indicated in caption by italics.

cover author's collection
ii author's collection
x Minnesota Historical Society
2 l&r WCHS collection
3 Minnesota Historical Society
4 Minnesota Historical Society
5 Minnesota Historical Society
6 Minnesota Historical Society
8 WCHS collection
10 WCHS collection
11 WCHS collection
12 WCHS collection
13 WCHS collection
15 WCHS collection
16 Jim Johnson collection
17 t&b WCHS collection
18 author's collection
19 courtesy Chuck Dougherty
21 WCHS collection
23 WCHS collection
25 courtesy Terry Giebler

26 courtesy Terry Giebler
28 WCHS collection
29 courtesy Glenn Goggin
31 courtesy Peter Zang
32 Minnesota Historical Society
33 Minnesota Historical Society
34 courtesy Simonet Furniture Company
35 courtesy Catherine Flynn
36 Minnesota Historical Society
37 WCHS collection
38 author's collection
40 WCHS collection
41 WCHS collection
42 l WCHS collection
42 r courtesy Evelyn Peterson
43 courtesy Evelyn Peterson
44 author's collection
45 WCHS collection
46 courtesy Images of the Past and Present, Lee Bjerk collection
47 courtesy Images of the Past and Present, Lee Bjerk collection
48 author's collection
49 WCHS collection
50 WCHS collection
52 WCHS collection
54 WCHS collection

55 WCHS collection
56 Minnesota Historical Society
58 l&r WCHS collection
60 WCHS collection
61 WCHS collection
63 l&r courtesy Roger Peterson
65 courtesy Roger Peterson
66 Minnesota Historical Society
67 Minnesota Historical Society
68 courtesy Darlene Schell Peterson
71 WCHS collection
72 courtesy Mark Crimmins
73 l&r WCHS collection
74 l&r WCHS collection
75 courtesy Darlene Schell Peterson
76 courtesy Images of the Past and Present, Lee Bjerk collection
77 Minnesota Historical Society
78 Minnesota Historical Society
79 Minnesota Historical Society
80 courtesy Catherine Flynn
83 WCHS collection
85 courtesy Ascension Episcopal Church, Stillwater

86 courtesy St. Paul Lutheran Church, Stillwater
87 courtesy Trinity Lutheran Church, Stillwater
88 author's collection
90 WCHS collection
91 WCHS collection
92 courtesy Images of the Past and Present, Lee Bjerk collection
93 author's collection
94 t2, ll WCHS collection
94 lr author's collection
95 WCHS collection
96 Minnesota Historical Society
97 l courtesy Mrs. Wilson Staples
97 r WCHS collection
98 author's collection
99 WCHS collection
100 Minnesota Historical Society
101 Minnesota Historical Society
102 l WCHS collection
102 r Minnesota Historical Society
103 Minnesota Historical Society

Bibliography

Buck, Anita A., *Steamboats on the St. Croix,* North Star Press, St. Cloud, Minnesota, 1990.

Easton, A.B., *The History of the St. Croix Valley,* two vols., H.C. Cooper & Co., Chicago, Illinois, 1909.

Johnston, Patricia C., *Stillwater: Minnesota's Birthplace in Photographs by John Runk,* Johnston Publishing Inc., Afton, Minnesota, 1980.

Independent School District #834 *Annual Report,* 1976.

Neill, Edward D., *History of Washington County and the St. Croix Valley,* North Star Publishing Co., Minneapolis, Minnesota, 1881.

Polk, R. L. & Co., *Stillwater City Directory,* 1890-present.

Pratt, George B., *The Valley of the St. Croix,* Art Pub;lishing Co., Neenah, Wisocnsin, 1888.

Washington County Historical Society, *Washington: A Histor of the County,* The Croixside Press, Stillwater, Minnesota, 1977.

Minnesota History, Volume 37, Number 4, "The Minnesota State Prison during the Stillwater Era, 1853-1914.," by James Taylor Dunn. December 1960, pp 137-151.

NEWSPAPERS

Prision Mirror, April 23, 1965, pp. 1.

St. Croix Union, 1854-

St. Paul *Pioneer Press,* 1931-1962.

Stillwater *Gazette* (Both Daily & Weekly), 1870-1982; also the special *Trade Times,* January 1898.

Stillwater *Messenger ,* Republican and *Post-Messenger,* 1856- .

Stillwater *Daily Sun,* 1881-1884.

Stillwater *Trade News,* 1935.

Stillwater *News,* 1920.

10 Index

A scene frozen in time. Myrtle Street between 3rd and 4th Streets. ca. 1904, *Frederick Neumeier.*
A boy pauses as his cow takes a sip.